REVELATORY

LANDSCAPES

REVELATORY

Kathryn Gustafson
Jaimi Baer +
Conger Moss Guillard
Landscape Architecture

Hargreaves Associates
in collaboration with
Julian Lang

Hood Design
in collaboration with
Olly Wilson +
Douglas Hollis

Tom Leader Studio
in collaboration with
Anuradha Mathur +
Dilip da Cunha

LANDSCAPES

San Francisco Museum of Modern Art

This catalogue is published on the occasion of the exhibition *Revelatory Landscapes,* organized by Aaron Betsky and Leah Levy at the San Francisco Museum of Modern Art and on view at the Museum and outdoor sites around the San Francisco Bay Area from May 5 to October 14, 2001.

This exhibition is made possible by grants from The Andy Warhol Foundation for the Visual Arts, The Creative Work Fund, the Graham Foundation for Advanced Studies in the Fine Arts, and the LEF Foundation.

Distributed by RAM Publications, 2525 Michigan Avenue, No. A2,
Santa Monica, California 90404

Library of Congress Cataloging-in-Publication Data:

Betsky, Aaron
Revelatory landscapes / Aaron Betsky, Leah Levy, Dean MacCannell
p. cm.
Includes bibliographical references.
ISBN 0-918471-64-8 (pbk.)
1. Landscape architecture—California—Exhibitions.
I. Levy, Leah. II. MacCannell, Dean. III. Title.

SB469.78.U6 B48 2001
712'.074'79461—dc21 2001032245

Revelatory Landscapes was produced by the Publications Department of the San Francisco Museum of Modern Art.
Kara Kirk, *Director of Publications and Graphic Design*
Alexandra Chappell, *Publications Coordinator*
Jason Goldman, *Publications Assistant*

Edited by Janet Wilson
Book and Jacket Design by Tenazas Design San Francisco
Revelatory Landscapes Installation Photography by Richard Barnes

Cover and inside cover:
Tom Leader Studio in collaboration with Anuradha Mathur and Dilip daCunha, *Coastlines*, 2001

Photography Credits
Cover, frontispiece, and pages 28–61: photographs © Richard Barnes

P. 9: © Estate of Robert Smithson/Licensed by VAGA, New York, NY. Photo by Gianfranco Gorgoni; p. 13: courtesy of the Gordon Matta-Clark Trust. Photo by Ben Blackwell; p. 15 (top): © Tim Street-Porter/Esto; p. 15 (bottom): photo by Margherita Spiluttini; p. 19: courtesy of ADOBE LA; p. 22: © Christo 1976. Photo by Jeanne-Claude; p. 23: courtesy of Tom Leader; p. 24: photo by John Gollings; p. 25: courtesy of Kathryn Gustafson.

Pp. 62–95: Unless otherwise noted here, all photographs are courtesy of the designer or design team whose work they represent. Pp. 62–65: © Luc Boegly; p. 66: photo by Amyn; p. 67 (top and bottom): © Nigel Young; pp. 70–71: © D. Finnin & R. Mickens/AMNH; pp: 76–77: photo by John Gollings; p. 78: courtesy of Olympic Coordination Authority; p. 79 (right): photo by John Gollings; p. 89: © Mimmo Capone, Rome; p. 94: photo by Bruce Dees and Assoc., Seattle; pp. 103–04: maps by James Williams.

TABLE OF CONTENTS

Foreword + Acknowledgments

David A. Ross *Director*

Since its founding in 1983, the San Francisco Museum of Modern Art's Department of Architecture and Design has presented materials documenting both built and visionary work by architects and landscape designers from around the globe. *Revelatory Landscapes* encompasses these two interests as they play out in the landscape and also marks the occasion of the museum's first off-site, outdoor exhibition. Several years in the making, the show presents the work of five innovative design teams that were commissioned to create site-specific installations at locations throughout the Bay Area. Each project merges a concern for the environment with the realization that the formed land reveals aspects of our social and cultural histories.

This exhibition was the product of a unique collaboration between the curators—Aaron Betsky, former SFMOMA curator of architecture, design, and digital projects, and Leah Levy, guest curator—and the design teams and their special partners in this undertaking: Kathryn Gustafson, working with architect Jaimi Baer and the firm of Conger Moss Guillard Landscape Architecture; George Hargreaves and Mary Margaret Jones, who worked with Native American linguist and poet Julian Lang; Walter Hood, who collaborated with jazz composer Olly Wilson and artist Douglas Hollis; Tom Leader, who worked with landscape planners Anuradha Mathur and Dilip da Cunha; and Gustavo Leclerc, Ulises Diaz, Barbara Jones, and Laura Alvarez of the collective ADOBE LA (an acronym for Architects, Artists, and Designers Opening the Border Edge of Los Angeles). We are indebted to all of these participants for their enthusiasm, creativity, and plain hard work, which are manifest in each of the resulting installations.

One of the five projects, ADOBE LA's *Red Is Out*, was not completed as scheduled and we regret that we were unable to include it in this publication, which documents the completed *Revelatory Landscapes* installations along with previous work by the lead designers. We are grateful to the individuals who contributed their talents and creativity to this catalogue, especially Janet Wilson, who edited the text; Lucille Tenazas, who designed its pages; and Richard Barnes, who photographed the site-specific installations.

The intricacy of this exhibition necessitated the assistance of many other collaborators, who are acknowledged individually on pages 103–4 of this volume. It also required the time and energy of a number of SFMOMA staff members: Michelle Barger, Robin Bernhard, Ruth Berson, Matt Biederman, Alexandra Chappell, Olga Charyshyn, Alexander Cheves, Steve Dye, Evan Forfar, Libby Garrison, Jason Goldman, Keiko Hayashi, John Holland, Ruth Keffer, Julie Kim, Sarah King, Kara Kirk, Kent Roberts, Jennifer Siekert, Cassandra Paras Smith, Paul Tavian, James Williams, and Greg Wilson. On behalf of the curators, special thanks are due to several individuals who over the years have generously shared their knowledge and expertise in the area of landscape design: Achva Stein, Marc Treib, and Peter Walker, principal, Peter Walker Partners, Berkeley. Alice Waters, Joy Natoli, and Bruce Wilcox merit thanks for their inspiring discussions about the nature of landscape. The complexity of planning for these site-specific installations required the assistance and cooperation of a number of other individuals, to whom we offer our thanks: Bhaman Sheik; Barbara

Kaufman and Leslie Lacko of the Bay Conservation and Development Commission; Amy Coburn and Elizabeth Wolff of Catellus Urban Development Corp.; Pedro Arce of the City and County of San Francisco Planning Department; Jill Manton of the San Francisco Arts Commission; and Tiffany Bohee and Amy Neches of the San Francisco Redevelopment Agency. The exhibition itself, as well as the materials created to document and interpret it—a brochure, a Web site, and this publication—would not have been possible without the generous assistance of a number of funders. We are indebted to The Andy Warhol Foundation for the Visual Arts, The Creative Work Fund, the Graham Foundation for Advanced Studies in the Fine Arts, and the LEF Foundation for grants in support of the *Revelatory Landscapes* project, which have enabled SFMOMA to explore this important new terrain.

Preface

Leah Levy *Guest Curator*
Aaron Betsky *Former Curator of Architecture, Design + Digital Projects*

Over the past quarter century, landscape architecture has undergone a major transition, moving beyond the planting and shaping of gardens and parks. Some of the best new landscape design is related to the earthworks created by postwar artists seeking to expose what exists on a site, revealing its essential nature, and making visible typically unseen landscape zones. These works focus our attention on the grittier, leftover places in the urban scene, where redevelopment creates fissures in the city's fabric, where earthquake faults open up space, and where long-standing infrastructure leaves us inured to its presence.

For *Revelatory Landscapes,* each of the design teams created a project that uncovers vestiges of a hidden history, culture, or physical attribute—the stuff of our collective memory. The exhibition encourages us to take the time for a fresh look at our surroundings, necessitating a pilgrimage of sorts to the installation sites in Berkeley, Oakland, San Jose, and San Francisco. What we find are actions on the land that frame, in subtle and memorable ways, a new perception of the world we inhabit.

These site projects connect us to the tradition of humankind's attempt to sculpt the land while encouraging us to reflect on the preoccupations of contemporary society. They engage and provoke us by means of the familiar, the abstract, and the enigmatic. They restate both an identification with and a disassociation from the notions of place, neighborhood, and land. While evoking formative experiences in the landscapes of our childhoods, they also acknowledge the environments we are responsible for making today. At the beginning of a new century, these works on the land could become a radical gesture, luring us out of the white box—whether home, office, or museum—and into the landscapes that shape our lives and our futures.

DIG WE MUST

An Argument for Revelatory Landscapes

Aaron Betsky

The land we inhabit is an accumulation of past events we can make visible by means of landscape architecture. That is the simple premise of this exhibition. It assumes that we think of the discipline of landscape architecture as involving not only the planting of certain forms of flora or the shaping of geography toward scenic ends but also the acts of digging, naming, articulating, and otherwise clarifying what already exists. This is not a question of telling some great truth. In digging and naming, landscape architecture alters the field on which it operates in such a manner that there is no question of a neutral act of making clear what already exists. Instead, the designer is able to reveal structures that exist only in the act of interpretation and making.

Revelatory landscape practices, stand in other words, are as much inventions as any other form of art. Their structures are fictions of the real that tell us stories about where we are and how we might understand our place in that physical world. It is only in the act of digging, marking, and otherwise removing, rather than adding, that revelatory landscapes are different from some other forms of landscape practice. They are a way of gathering together into unconcealment a world that we otherwise barely notice so that we can stand witness to what we are.[1]

1 | I use this phrase in the manner proposed by Martin Heidegger in *The Question Concerning Technology and Other Essays*, trans. by William Lovitt (New York: Harper & Row, 1977), to indicate the revelation of that which is already always around us.

Revelatory landscape practices stand in contrast to most of the history of landscape architecture. We think of this discipline as primarily concerned with the making of gardens, and this is generally true. Landscape architecture is distinguished from agriculture or other forms of productive reformations of the land by the addition of formal elements designed to shape our experience or interpretation of the site. Such formal systems are primarily visual (although smell obviously plays an important role in some garden design, as do the other senses) and were, until the eighteenth century, defined by geometry. Gardens existed at the intersection of an abstract ordering system imposed on the land and the manner in which things grow, water falls, and forces such as wind and gravity affect the appearance of things.[2]

2 | The locus classicus for the discussion of such theories is Rudolf Wittkower's *Architectural Principles in the Age of Humanism* (New York: W. W. Norton, 1971). See also Alberto Pérez-Gómez, *Architecture and the Crisis of Modern Science* (Cambridge,Mass.: MIT Press, 1983).

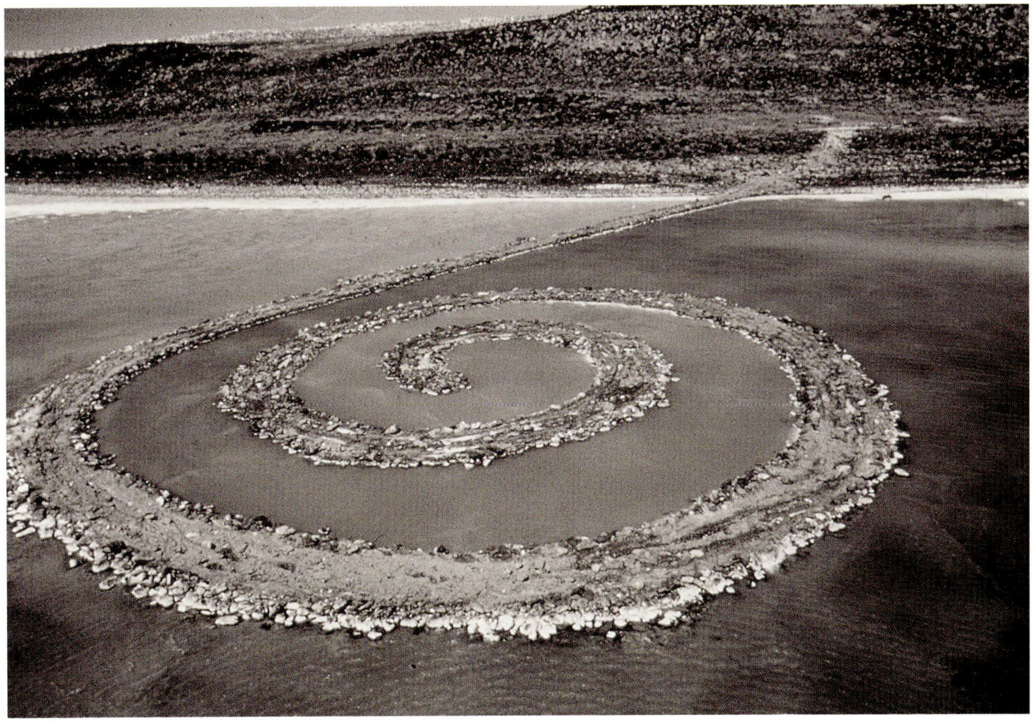

FIGURE 1 Robert Smithson, *Spiral Jetty*, 1970
Collection Dia Center for the Arts, New York
Estate of Robert Smithson, courtesy of
James Cohan Gallery, New York

What has always distinguished landscape architecture from other forms of art making is its continual reality. Things always change and are always contingent in a landscape, no matter how severe the geometry, clear the vista, or grand the scheme by which nature is trained to human purposes. Whereas most other forms of art abstract not only the system but also the material of appearance, landscape architecture has to accept the organic development of its subject as an intrinsic part of its task.[3] While architecture is both present and represents,[4] it is (relatively) immutable and, by its very nature, a human artifice, thus alien to the primary condition of the land. Once built, it remains the same, which is to say alien to the site. Landscape architecture operates within that primary site.[5]

Landscape architecture, in other words, has never been able to remove itself from the development of space in time. Because of the simple fact that things grow, die, and change in ways that we can husband but never fully control, a garden or shaped land area changes continually, both in a linear and a cyclical manner. Even more than architecture, it remains rooted in a time-based reality that no manner of training or abstraction can completely deny. We can even see it as defining the very limits of art as human artifice, in that it is ultimately a restaging of what exists in a manner that reveals the hand of the maker but remains, by its very nature, always part of what we think of as the opposite of art, that is, nature.

3 | It is interesting to note that landscape architects have not developed a theory of "organic" design to match that of architects. Instead, landscape theory has split itself off from consumer-oriented ideas espoused in books published by presses such as Rodale on how gardens grow.

4 | Mario Gandelsonas pointed out this quality of architecture in "From Structure to Subject: The Formation of an Architectural Language," in Peter Eisenman, *House X* (New York: Rizzoli International Publications, 1982), 7–31.

5 | For a case study in the artificiality of the garden see Denise Le Dantec and Jean-Pierre Le Dantec, *Reading the French Garden: Story and History* (Cambridge, Mass.: MIT Press, 1990). See also Monique Mosser and Georges Teyssot, eds., *The Architecture of Western Gardens: A Design History from the Renaissance to the Present* (Cambridge, Mass.: MIT Press, 1991); Charles W. Moore, William J. Mitchell, and William Turnbull, Jr., *The Poetics of Gardens* (Cambridge, Mass.: MIT Press, 1988).

Just as architecture almost disappears into construction, and painting into representation (even if only of representation itself), landscape architecture has always threatened to disappear into the land itself. This has certainly been true ever since it confronted this contradiction in the era of Capability Brown. Its ruses became ever more sophisticated as it sought to dissolve its tricks and systems into the land itself. From the hidden ditches that turned sheep meadows into lawns to the berms that let the turning radius of the automobile carve its path through geography, landscape architecture has found ever more recourse to those tools that would have it dissolve into the land itself.

The notion of the natural and the human fusing into a seamless experience has been landscape architecture's greatest myth. It has led to its greatest triumphs. The most notable of these were the public parks of the late nineteenth century, when human technology and natural form came together into stage sets of and in the real. Such places covered up all discrepancies between who we are, what we make, and where we live by assigning us a place in a bucolic Arcadian vision. That this was a complete artifice mattered less than the complete nature of accomplishments such as New York's Central Park.[6]

While the mainstream of landscape architecture continues to be concerned with such effects, that segment of the discipline we might regard as a (self) critical practice has attempted to make a case for itself at the very point where it seemed to disappear into engineering or decoration. It has become either the making of roads, waterways, leech fields, remediation fields, or retaining walls, or it has become instances of intricate and self-referential form making that usually exists as a fringe around buildings. While the traditions of both gardens and parks live on, they are of increasingly less concern to landscape architecture as an active discipline operating at the self-explanatory and thus relatively artless intersection of ordering devices and natural forms.[7]

What has most recently invigorated the profession is an awareness of three elements: the accumulation of human acts as forming what might be considered a secondary nature nearly indistinguishable from the first or original one; the emergence of land, or site-specific art as a way of re-creating that meeting place of order and site; and the awareness that shaping the land can be a way of restoring or remaking visible geological constructs, climate patterns, and ecosystems. It is out of cultural criticism (or material culture research), forms of monumental art making, and a sense of ecological stewardship that landscape architecture has found a new lease on life.

6 | Frederick Law Olmsted, Central Park's designer, is once again the subject of great interest. See Witold Rybczynski, *A Clearing in the Distance: Frederick Law Olmsted and America in the Nineteenth Century* (New York: Scribners, 1999).

7 | For a good description of the relationship between landscape and infrastructure, see Christian Zapata, *The American Landscape* (New York: Princeton Architectural Press, 1995).

Revelatory landscape practices, in other words, are as much inventions as any other form of art. Their structures are fictions of the real that tell us stories about where we are and how we might understand our place in that physical world.

The first of these wellsprings was most clearly articulated, at least in the United States, by the landscape historian J. B. Jackson. In his writings on the vernacular aspects of landscape, he made it clear that the accumulation of agricultural techniques, patterns of ownership, building types, and the contingency of various reactions to events combined to create a landscape in which that which grows, that which appears because of geological or climatological forces, and that which humans have made and continue to make cannot be readily separated. It is up to the landscape architect (as well as the architect or planner) to operate in this field. In doing so, they must realize that their artifices are just rearticulations of standard types and responses to either human or natural conditions that will be repeated, reformulated, and buried by further reactions to the land.[8]

In England at the turn of the last century, Patrick Geddes had come to much of the same conclusion. His work consisted, however, in a historical reading of cities that was meant to show how the relationship between natural resources and conditions, their use, and the subsequent forms continually layered upon one another create a set of always changing landscapes of daily experience. He saw design as an extension of surveying these conditions. The aim of the designer was not to impose new and supposedly more rational forms on this accumulation of form but rather to work with these facts on the ground to create cities that could provide places of habitation, public enjoyment, free movement, and productive space. The new might be no more than an articulation and extension of what already exists. It is a manner of thinking that has been fundamental in shaping urban design policies throughout the world, especially in northern Europe.[9]

While such critics looked at the reality of the land, what we now call "land art" was first practiced in the early 1960s, in a way we would recognize today, by Robert Smithson.[10] His massive projects not only added geometric form to the land but also criticized the very nature of the site. Smithson saw his work as a continuation of the memory of place, the act of finding form in the detritus of what man has made, and a critique of such conditions. By pouring asphalt over dirt, he turned the act of paving into a form of sculpture, and with *Spiral Jetty* (1970, fig. 1), he turned the engineering of water control back onto itself. His work was useless and not pretty. It abstracted the land while making it more immediately present and visceral. The real world was as much an act of apperception and interpretation coming into form, Smithson posed, as it was something that we could shape to please ourselves.[11]

8 | John Brinckerhoff Jackson, *A Sense of Place, a Sense of Time* (New Haven and London: Yale University Press, 1994); Dean MacCannell, "The Common Landscape after John Brinckerhoff Jackson," *Design Book Review*, no. 40 (Fall 1999): 50–56.

9 | Cf. Volker M. Welter, *Biopolis: Patrick Geddes and the City of Life* (Cambridge, Mass.: MIT Press, 2001); Volker M. Welter and James Lawson, eds., *The City of Patrick Geddes* (Oxford, New York: Peter Lang Publishing, 2000). To put Geddes in a historical context, see Bernard Colenbrander, *De Verstrooide Stad* (Rotterdam: NAi Publishers, 1999).

10 | The classic definition of such work is that of John Beardsley in his *Earthworks and Beyond: Contemporary Art in the Landscape* (New York: Abbeville Press, 1998). See also Jeffrey Kastner, ed., *Land and Environmental Art* (London: Phaidon Press, 1998).

11 | Cf. Robert Hobbs, *Robert Smithson: Sculpture* (Ithaca, N.Y.: Cornell University Press, 1981); Gary Shapiro, *Earthwards: Robert Smithson and Art after Babel* (Berkeley: University of California Press, 1997).

Several generations of land-based artists have built on this opening to develop what Rosalind Krauss has called the "expanded field" of sculpture.[12] Their experiments have ranged from the construction of monumental, uninhabitable cities that nobody ever sees (Michael Heizer) to the construction of small insertions in the landscape through which fragments of order appear (Mary Miss). At their grandest, these artworks aspire to cosmological systems that make the inherent order of the land itself visible or perceptible (James Turrell, Walter de Maria).[13] By now fully integrated into the practices of such designers as Peter Walker and George Hargreaves, these forms of art making have reshaped our notion of the land.

Ecological concerns, finally, are the most recent influences on landscape architecture. They date to the era following the oil crisis of 1973, but have roots in earlier efforts to see gardens as ways of creating self-sufficient and free communities. Tinged by a utopian belief in the ability of technology to save us from the excesses of our past application of tools and machinery, this form of land reclamation has also developed into a dance of flood- and erosion-control devices. Its designers seek to accept the nature of things and delight in the eminently responsible and responsive forms they create. Starting from a reaction to the channelization of rivers and destruction of wetlands, an ecologically oriented landscape architecture has moved into speculations about the ways in which we can shape the land to leech poison out of its furrows or harness wind to create places of habitation. Here aesthetic and scientific concerns merge in the belief that, while we engage in aggressive interventions in the land, in the end we should just let nature make forms and then adapt ourselves to the results.[14]

Most recently, such influences have come together and been reinterpreted by thinkers such as James Corner and Allen Weiss, who have pointed out the continuing artificiality of all such "un-design" efforts. They have argued that the acts of mapping and describing in and of themselves alter our experience of space and that, through techniques of describing, rather than self-conscious making, we might be able to find landscapes of revelation. According to Corner,

> **Avoiding the failure of universalist approaches toward master-planning and the imposition of state-controlled schemes, the unfolding agency of mapping may allow designers and planners not only to see certain possibilities in the complexity and contradiction of what already exists, but also to actualize that potential.**[15]

12 | Rosalind Krauss, "Sculpture in the Expanded Field," *October,* no. 8 (1979): 58–64.

13 | Such work has obviously occurred within the realm and according to the standards of fine arts. For the influence of such work on current landscape practices, see Udo Weilacher, *Between Landscape Architecture and Land Art,* trans. by Felicity Goth (Basel: Birkhäuser Verlag, 1999).

14 | Cf. John Tillman Lyle, *Design for Human Ecosystems: Landscape, Land Use, and Natural Resources* (Washington D.C.: Island Press, 1999); Ken Yeang, *Designing with Nature: The Ecological Basis for Architectural Design* (New York: McGraw-Hill, 1995).

15 | James Corner, "The Agency of Mapping," 212, in Denis Cosgrove, ed. *Mappings* (London: Reaktion Books, 1999): 211–300.

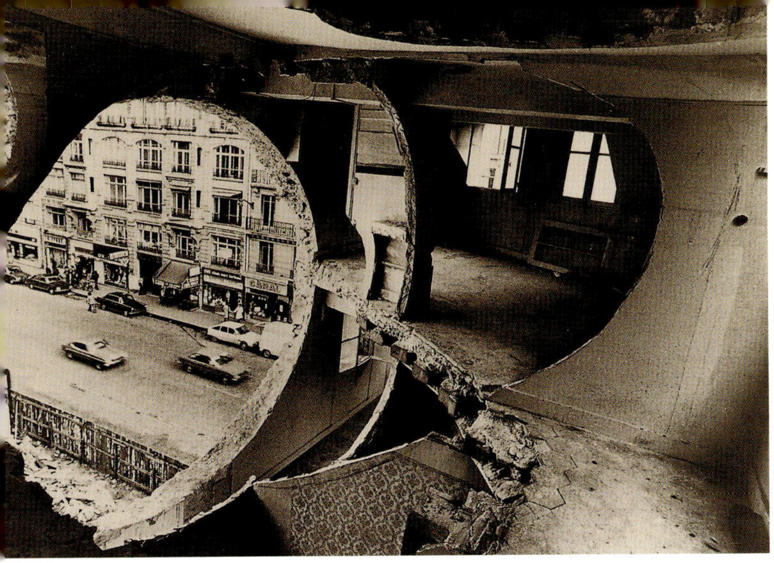

FIGURE 2 Gordon Matta-Clark, *Conical Intersect*, 1975 Collection of the San Francisco Museum of Modern Art. Accessions Committee Fund: gift of Frances and John Bowes, Pam and Dick Kramlich, Collectors Forum, and the Modern Art Council, 92.426

Weiss has pointed out that gardens might be "subversive" by confusing what is built, what is natural, what is real, and what is mimesis:

> **At the end of the twentieth century, a certain type of garden would seem to be in constant revolt against both the restrictions of *mathesis* (universal or otherwise) and those of *mimesis:* a garden that is not "natural," yet one that permits the apparition of nature; a marginal garden.**[16]

To both of these thinkers, the artifice of landscape lies in the awareness of its unnaturalness. It is up to the landscape architect to pose interpretations, not necessarily interventions. By staying within the realm of representation, landscape architecture can be a form of cultural criticism. Whether as perspectival constructs or metaphorical scrims, landscape forms as abstract organizing devices continue to exercise a certain control of the land, but they now also serve as self-conscious acts of critical interpretation. Landscape architecture reduces itself only to a new way of knowing what is already there.

Although I would agree that this is the logical end point of an interpretation of the history of landscape architecture, I would also argue that a new avenue is possible to the—quite literal—opening of the land. It is what I would term the "Matta-Clarking" of the landscape. Derived from the work of the artist Gordon Matta-Clark, it proposes a form of "un-building" that consists of acts of removal, marking, and naming that create a definite and positive—if sometimes nonoccupiable—space. Developed by architects such as Frank Gehry during the 1980s, this form of revelatory design practice does not merely make visible what is already there, but acts to open up and let us experience what is not there until we actually participate in the act of making.

Though he engaged in a variety of site-specific actions and constructs, Gordon Matta-Clark's most famous work consisted of cutting open existing buildings. This intervention altered the existing structures, causing them to sag or otherwise rearrange their physical properties, usually toward compaction. At the same time, a new space emerged: the V-shape of *Splitting* (1974), the ovoid of *Day's End* (1975), and the spiral of *Conical Intersect* (1975, fig. 2). These spaces were negative or void, yet they managed to convey a sense of being figures whose abstract clarity stood in contrast to the convolutions of the forms all around them.[17]

16 | Allen S. Weiss, *Unnatural Horizons: Paradox and Contradiction in Landscape Architecture* (New York: Princeton Architectural Press, 1998), 153. See also Hal Foster, *The Return of the Real: The Avant-Garde at the Turn of the Century* (Cambridge, Mass.: MIT Press, 1996).

17 | Cf. Mary Jane Jacob, *Gordon Matta-Clark: A Retrospective* (Chicago: Museum of Contemporary Art, Chicago, 1985); Corinne Diserens, *Gordon Matta-Clark* (Marseille: Musées de Marseille, 1993).

Such interventions made the leftover detritus of industrial buildings or no-longer-occupied homes seem pregnant with form while drawing our attention to their remaining bits and pieces as objects in and of themselves. Beginning in the early 1970s, Frank Gehry started to work from the other side of the equation, declaring that "a building under construction is much more beautiful than once it is finished."[18] For this architect, the building blocks of structures, rather than their finished forms, were filled with the potential of form that we usually bury inside our completed habitations. He pursued this line of reasoning by partially undressing his own house in Santa Monica (1978) and elaborating on half-finished construction in the Venice Beach Spiller House of 1982 (fig. 3).[19]

While Gehry was content (at least for a while) to let unfinished buildings speak for themselves, architects such as Eric Owen Moss delighted in an almost baroque posing and elaboration of found fragments. Moss also cut holes in buildings, revealing the existing structure, but then he would elaborate what he had found into fantastic, spiraling constructions that often took on forms all their own.[20] By contrast, New Mexico–based architect Antoine Predock became interested in buildings as accumulations of detritus ("road cuts," as he called them, that revealed the history of a place's geographic and human transformations), but he expressed such findings in the smooth surfaces of concrete and stucco.[21]

A parallel influence on the reuse and rearticulation of the built environment was the work of Joseph Beuys, who delighted in his shamanistic ability to give meaning to objects through collecting and displaying them.[22] Rescuing fragments of "dead tech" and the landscape, he gave a mythic meaning to a world in which what was real and what was invented could not be separated, thereby opening a new era of landscape painting in the work of Sigmar Polke and Anselm Kiefer. Meanwhile, artists such as Jan Dibbets were content to merely turn the land into an artwork by measuring and photographing that act.[23]

A whole other generation of architects has been more interested in the naming and marking of sites through construction. Peter Eisenman's resurrection of an armory that once stood on the site of his Wexner Center for the Arts at Ohio State University (1988) is a signal example of such activities. He continued his partial reconstruction and built mappings throughout the 1980s, although it has now become clear that the sheer complexity of such structures tends to obscure more than reveal.[24] Perhaps more productive are the experiments performed by the Swiss architects Jacques Herzog and Pierre de Meuron. Accepting sites and constraints, they twist basic plot forms into structures that become sculptural markers. The

18 | As quoted in Peter Arnell, "No, I Am Not an Architect: Frank Gehry and Peter Arnell: A Conversation," 13, in Frank O. Gehry, *Frank Gehry: Buildings and Projects* (New York: Rizzoli International Publications, 1985), 13–18.

19 | For the best survey of the work of this period, see Gehry, *Frank Gehry*. Since then, Gehry has largely abandoned this approach to architecture.

20 | This is especially true of early works such as the Paramount Laundry Building (1989) and 8522 National Boulevard (1990). See Eric Owen Moss, *Eric Owen Moss: Buildings and Projects* (New York: Rizzoli International Publications, 1991).

21 | See Antoine Predock, *Antoine Predock: Buildings and Projects* (New York: Rizzoli International Publications, 1994); Antoine Predock, *Antoine Predock 2* (New York: Rizzoli International Publications, 1999).

22 | Beuys obviously had a tremendous influence on those extending the notion of art as a combination of site-specific and performance art. See Alain Burer, *The Essential Joseph Beuys*, ed. Lothar Schirmer (Cambridge, Mass.: MIT Press, 1997).

23 | Cf. R. H. Fuchs and M. M. M. Vos, *Jan Dibbets* (Minneapolis: Walker Art Center; New York: Rizzoli International Publications, 1987).

24 | Cf. Peter Eisenman, *Wexner Center for the Visual Arts, The Ohio State University* (New York: Rizzoli International Publications, 1989).

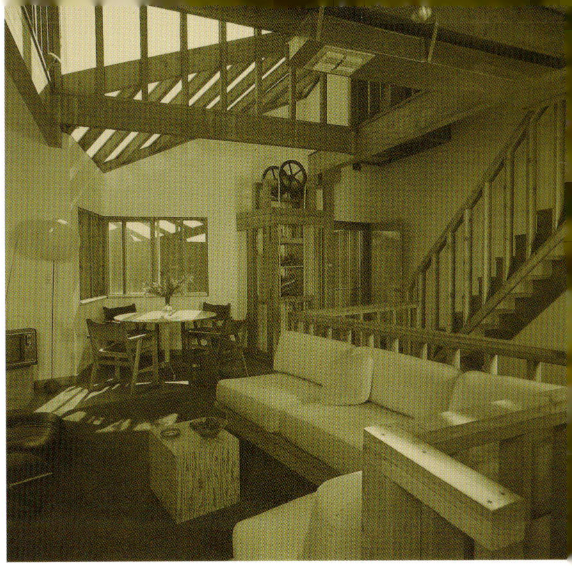

FIGURE 3 Frank Gehry, Spiller House, Venice Beach, 1982
Photo by Tim Street-Porter/Esto

clearest example of this technique is their Central Signal Tower in Basel (1999, fig. 4). They also let mold grow on building facades they have treated with certain chemical agents, mimic shadows with printed patterns, cover buildings with photographic images, and in general begin to see their structures as engaged in an active relationship with things that grow or drift onto a site. They do not evoke natural conditions so much as they mark the nature of human intervention in what might still be called nature.[25]

There is, of course, a long tradition of archaeology as a way of teaching us about ourselves. The Renaissance was, at least in part, rooted in the myth that a new society could emerge out of resurrecting what had been buried, and we continue to be fascinated with the notion of lost and buried worlds that might hold the key to our future.[26] I would argue that here resides the notion of utopia, so necessary as a countermodel to quotidian malaise—not as pie in the sky or in some indeterminate future, but hidden and sublimated in the everyday, waiting to be revealed within the fabric of daily life.[27]

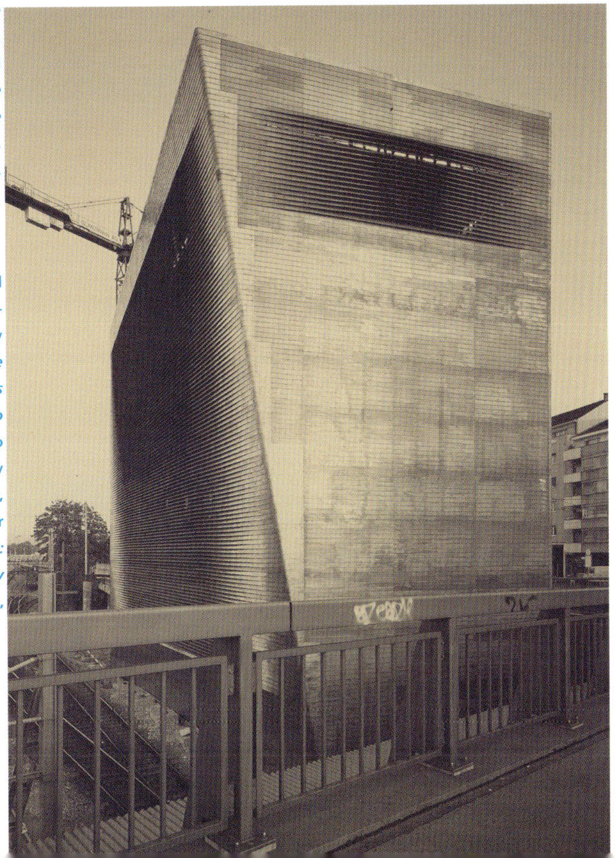

FIGURE 4 Herzog & de Meuron, *Central Signal Tower*, Basel, 1999
Photo by Margherita Spiluttini

25 Cf. Wilfried Wang, *Herzog and de Meuron* (Basel: Birkhäuser Verlag, 1998).

26 The very word Renaissance implies a rebirth of classical civilization. For the manner in which the cult of archaeology later influenced the development of architecture and planning, see Joseph Rykwert, *The First Moderns: The Architects of the Eighteenth Century* (Cambridge, Mass.: MIT Press, 1980), and Anthony Vidler, *The Writing of the Walls: Architectural Theory in the Late Enlightenment* (Princeton, N.J.: Princeton Architectural Press, 1987).

27 The confluence of architectural utopias and dread of the suppressed was first explored by Manfredo Tafuri in *The Sphere and the Labyrinth: Avant-Gardes and Architecture from Piranesi to the 1970s*, trans. by Pellegrino d'Acierno and Robert Connolly (Cambridge, Mass.: MIT Press, 1987), and later by Anthony Vidler in *The Architectural Uncanny: Essays in the Modern Unhomely* (Cambridge, Mass.: MIT Press, 1992).

This welter of investigation and ways of making art or architecture add up to a multipart model for a revelatory landscape. Although it is not clear whether landscape architects have consciously assimilated any of these techniques, it certainly appears possible that an analogous attitude toward the land might be productive. This kind of revelation has occurred in such European parks as the Parc de la Villette in Paris, where Alain Chimicoff revealed the sewage pipes coursing underneath the pleasure grounds, and in Peter Latz's ongoing project to transform the industrial wastelands of Duisburg, Germany, into parks. Thus far however, landscape architects have been less interested in the specifics of how landforms resulting from the interaction of accumulated human interventions and natural forces might react to incisions that could reveal their disparate parts. Instead, they have been content to point toward natural flows and to posit human interventions as sculptural artifacts.[28]

I would argue that adopting the technique of Matta-Clarking—or the ways of Beuys, Gehry, or any other investigators of the land—might offer a way for landscape to reveal its internal structure and material while offering an occupiable space. The current project initiated by the San Francisco Museum of Modern Art may offer some clues to pathways toward such forms of landscape practice.[29] Obviously there is a dual romanticism in this practice: one emanating from the love of that which is past and ruined or unused and that emanating from the belief that we can make a better place. The art here is never a true revelation of what exists, but an invention that resides in the manner of cutting or opening, the choice of what to reveal, and the designers' reaction to the results in built or shaped form. It glorifies what is no longer useful and is hopeful about what might take place in the future while realizing the act of the artist in a thoroughly contingent, but self-effacing, manner.

Similarly, the technique of marking and playing off natural and human systems in such a way that their most basic relationships become revealed is a dangerous rhetorical game. It presupposes an absolute quality to both what is real (natural) and what is invented (human). In the end, it proposes that, through the revelation of this difference, which is inherently an invention or our form of defining ourselves as separate from the world, some basic truth, even if one only apprehended, might stand out. Failing that, it contents itself with the pure pleasure of marking that itself creates a new ordering system on the land.

28 | For a useful survey of recent landscapes, see Sutherland Lyall, *Designing the New Landscape* (London: Thames & Hudson, 1998).

29 | As this essay has been written several months before the completion of the projects for this exhibition, I cannot say whether these works are fully engaged in revelatory landscape practices, but I believe that this undertaking in itself may articulate some facets of such methods of designing landscapes.

The art here is never a true revelation of what exists, but an invention that resides in the manner of cutting or opening, the choice of what to reveal, and the designers' reaction to the results in built or shaped form.

What, then, would be the purpose of revelatory landscape practices? Perhaps we can discern a meaning in these works if they are understood as a continual process of investigation that by its very activity poses questions about the reality of the land, what we have made of it, what we can know about it, and what our place on it might be. That is not to say that this is merely "process art."[30] The results of the investigations, the remains of days of digging, are themselves the things to be looked at. They are as much art as any bed of flowers or a contoured hill. They are as natural a result of landscape practice as the planting of a tree or the berming of a meadow. They can be as effective at evoking the pleasure and questions of the land as any more traditional practice. I would argue that they are more effective at making us aware of what is already there. What they can most definitely do is invite further revelations of ourselves as both users and practitioners of the landscape.

30 By this I mean art that produces not a final product but is an event or process in itself, thus merging with performance art but leaving a remainder or detritus behind to be exhibited or collected.

Landscape Architecture's Time

Dean MacCannell

Today some of the more interesting responses to problems of subjectivity, representation, collective memory, nature, and culture are being worked out in the landscape. This is being done by artists who employ dirt and by landscape architects who work conceptually. A pressing critical task is to catch up with the new thinking about self and place that is emerging from the current convergence of landscape design and art. The curatorial impetus for the San Francisco Museum of Modern Art's Revelatory Landscapes exhibition is the advancement of this new thought. For centuries, art has been the mode of human self-understanding that contains an opening for its own future subversion. Now perhaps it is landscape architecture's time to join with art in this crucial endeavor.

Until the middle of the twentieth century, landscape architecture sought inspiration by looking backward through history. The elegant geometric abstraction of Renaissance landscape design was intended as an application of Platonic forms. Nineteenth-century archaeology yielded layers of ancient environmental works that became models for romantic and nationalistic landscape design. The Beaux-Arts revival in the early twentieth century imported classical symmetries and details into large-scale designs for world's fairs and for the City Beautiful movement.

Landscape architecture's decisive rejection of styles from the past draws strength from two main sources. The first was a series of articles in the journal *Pencil Points* by Garret Eckbo, Daniel Kiley, and James Rose.[1] These pioneers of modernism theorized a break with the past and a new landscape based on human needs, the character of the natural environment, and the fit between them. From the casual elegance of the new California garden to A. E. Bye's delineation of the mood of a site, modernist landscape practice explored social and emotional contours beyond the reach of traditional design. High modernist landscape design never quite lived up to its promise to reflect the inner self or to resonate with deep sensibilities. It did, however, initiate a chaotic dialogue in which the self occasionally collides with things that are entirely intimate and entirely other—postmodernity.

1 The articles by Eckbo, Kiley, and Rose began appearing in the late 1930s. Their intervention, sometimes called the Harvard Revolution, ushered in the modern period in landscape design.

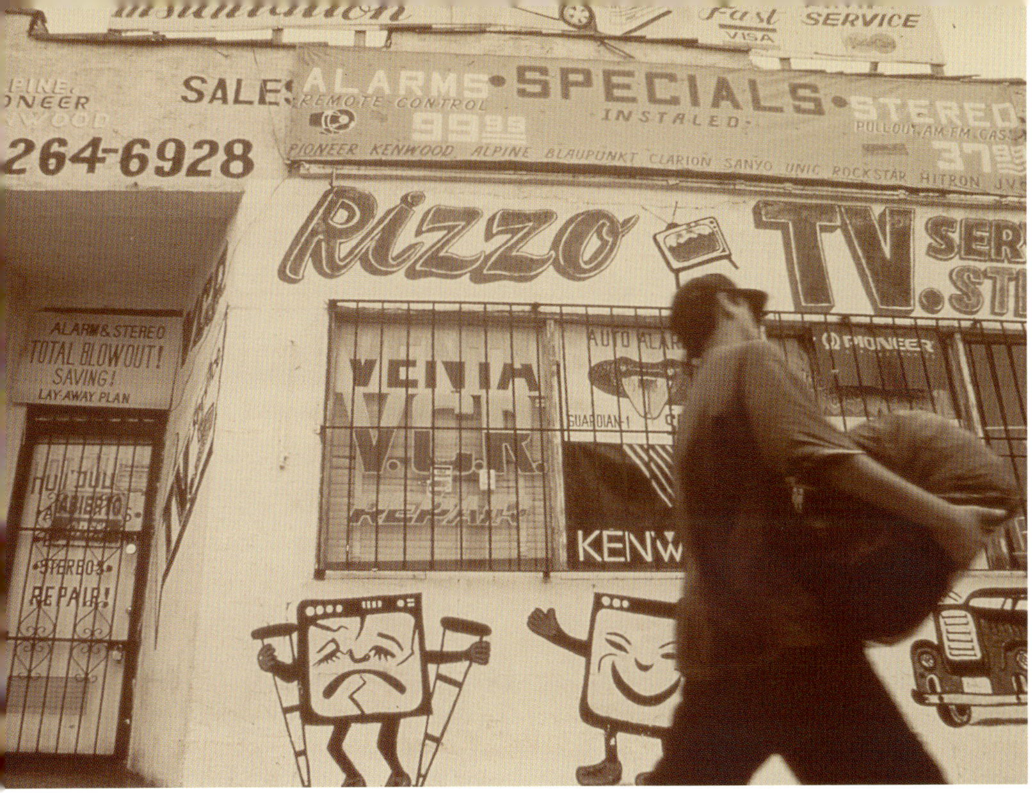

FIGURE 5 ADOBE LA (Gustavo Leclerc, Ulises Diaz, Alessandra Moctezuma, Julie Easton), *Sad TV/Happy TV*, from the series *Heterotopias of Latino L.A.* 1992–99

Beginning in the 1950s, the second contribution to a new landscape sensibility was J. B. Jackson's privileging of the design know-how contained in the routine practices of everyday life. His ability to see the love ordinary people put into shaping their worlds challenged all of us to think outside the conventions of design disciplines. After J. B. Jackson, landscape architects and designers began to understand what dramatists have always known—that everyday life is an inexhaustible resource for character, dignity, competence, emotion, meaning, knowledge, and new functional and aesthetic forms. This comes through very clearly in projects by the artists' and architects' collective ADOBE LA. Their photographic documentation of Los Angeles explores everyday expressive practices, including religious and commercial vernacular signage, body art, event posters, graffiti, and gang writing (fig. 5). The result is a series of beautiful images of a living landscape made of "hard work, stubborn hope, and mutual forbearance striving to be love."[2]

Landscape and Critical Theory

In what follows, I will engage certain aesthetics that might be called "postmodern," while eschewing the kind of criticism that goes by that name. The idea of "revelatory landscapes" runs counter to a mantra of postmodern criticism, namely, that "there is no longer a dialectic of surface and depth; there is nothing but a play of surfaces."[3] Fredric Jameson's aphoristic inauguration of postmodern criticism does not name a historical event, epoch, or horizon. It goes only so far as to name a point of view on history. Against the grain of postmodern criticism, I will proceed on the assumption that the existence of a surface means there is something underneath. If for no other reason than to release the energy and intelligence of the new landscape architecture, it is still worth asking, What is hidden, or buried, in the landscape? What remains to be revealed?

2 John Brinckerhoff Jackson, *Discovering the Vernacular Landscape* (New Haven: Yale University Press, 1984), xii.

3 Fredric Jameson, "Postmodernism or the Cultural Logic of Late Capitalism," *New Left Review* 146 (July-August 1984): 58.

After modernism, and after J. B. Jackson, landscape experimentation has come to understand itself as occupying the same ground as many other realms of inquiry: semiotics, language, ritual, myth, art, and psychoanalytic criticism of authority. What do these have in common with one another and with the landscape? They are the stuff that goes between and comes between human beings. Most of these intrasubjective realms are fully dependent upon collective agreement or fantasy. Speech is inherently empty. Authority as such is missing from the original human relationship. In order for language and authority to exert any force, we must collectively fill in what they lack. We must agree to the arbitrary conventions of speech while trying to infuse it with the strength that is missing. We must imagine authority and submit ourselves to it. Our common humanity is a collaborative work in progress imbued with a sense of pure possibility based on the ultimate absence of meaning and authority other than that which we collectively make up as we go along.

Within the intrahuman domain, landscape occupies a privileged position. J. B. Jackson once called the landscape "the image of our common humanity," which is a hopeful starting place.[4] Following Jackson's lead, I would suggest that landscape concretizes all the other intrasubjective orders. It is not absent—it is present in every human exchange. We don't need to make it up. Whether by design or not, it is already there between us and around us. It is the "third term" that gives shape and meaning to every other object and event. The power of the landscape to bestow meaning operates mainly at a preconscious or unconscious level. Except for the rare masterwork (that of J. B. Jackson first among them) and a few prepackaged neurotic banalities ("It is pretty," "It is well-kept," etc.), we refuse to engage the constitutive power of landscapes. Thus the idea of a revelatory landscape requires a double uncovering: first, the landscape itself, which we ordinarily distance from consciousness, and, second, the specific intrasubjective complexities that a landscape engenders.

Let me provide an example, which happens to be the oldest and therefore the simplest one. Consider a nightscape. It is a dark alley punctuated at intervals by cones of light from overhead street lamps. The sidewalk appears as a sequence of equal areas of light and dark. Each of these patches of light and dark is, say, twenty paces across. Now introduce human action into the scene. Three men pass through the alley. The first man takes his time, walking slowly in the light, but then increases his pace, moving quickly through the darkness. A few minutes later a second man passes. He moves slowly and deliberately in the darkness, and when he comes to the light, he speeds up, scampering quickly to the next patch of darkness. Then a third man passes. His pace through the alley is steady, indifferent to the alternation of light and dark.

4 John Brinckerhoff Jackson, *Discovering the Vernacular Landscape*, xii.

This scene is composed of the most elementary differentiation of the landscape into light and dark, and time, the pace of footsteps, fast and slow. Yet, for all its simplicity, we cannot prevent a drama from unfolding, with clear attributions of motive and character. The first man who hurries through the dark is fearful; the second, suspicious, probably a criminal with something to hide; and the third is cool, an existentialist, perhaps the hard-boiled detective who is trying to prevent a crime from being committed.

The production of meaning is fully dependent on the differentiations of the landscape—the most fundamental element of any landscape. Differentiation takes the form of edges, boundaries, paths, juxtapositions of built elements and plantings, or groupings of plants of different color, size, and texture. Light and dark provide the oldest differentiation. Separating light from darkness was the first division made by the God who took on the project of building the Garden of Eden. The second separation was sky and water, the third, earth from water, then plants, animals, birds, and eventually man and woman. The garden was the original background of human drama, the scene, setting, *Umwelt* for original human existence. From almost the very beginning, landscape has been the primary resource for fateful tests of personality and character. Character may seem to oscillate around a virtual center we call "identity." As background, the landscape is instrumental, even causal, to the way we understand character and identity. The scene tugs at us and makes us its subjects. It is where we appear that ineluctably shapes who we appear to be. The Ojibway people say that "land stands up for language—land supports what we say." The specific influence of the landscape is rarely grasped so succinctly. Ordinarily it operates as an invisible subjectivity hiding as landscape and waiting to be revealed.

Even in the simple example given above, a witness to the men in the alley would tend to project meaning onto human behavior and ignore the landscape as the coproducer of meaning. Dialectically, just as we assume authority where it doesn't exist, we discount the landscape because it is, or can be, much too present in our lives, even scary, acting within us but as another consciousness beyond our control. Very often what is most accessible to the human mind is also what it least understands—for example, the operation of the mind itself. And the landscape.

New Landscape Experimentation: Playing with Difference

The grounds of meaning production in the landscape are its differentiations: light and dark, nature and culture, past and present, object and representation. Some of the most interesting recent landscape experiments disrupt conventional oppositions in the landscape. Tom Leader's dunegrass piece at Longacres Park in Washington State (1994, fig. 6) plays with the kinds of oppositions and edges found in nature, but in a way that refers to itself as design. It is inspired by nature but does not strictly imitate it, focusing instead on an analysis of the colors, lines, and textures found in nature.

Christo and Jeanne-Claude's *Running Fence, Sonoma and Marin Counties, California, 1972–76* (fig. 7) was another landscape art project that called into question the ways we divide the landscape culturally along property lines. After negotiating with fifty-nine rural landowners in northern California, Christo and Jeanne-Claude built an eighteen-foot-tall fence of nylon fabric panels, steel poles, and cables that ran across the landscape in gentle curves for twenty-four and a half miles, sometimes following contours and sometimes not, but never honoring property lines. It was an antifence that united landowners with one another and with the land rather than dividing them. It inscribed an impossible arbitrary division in the landscape in order to make it an object. This kind of work reveals the subjective potential of landscape by calling into question the tendency to take it, and the meaning it usually engenders, for granted.

Disrupting conventional oppositions should heighten our appreciation of the differentiations of the landscape. We are creatures condemned to live our lives in culture, that is, in a world of meanings based on differences: dark and light, men and women, evil and good,

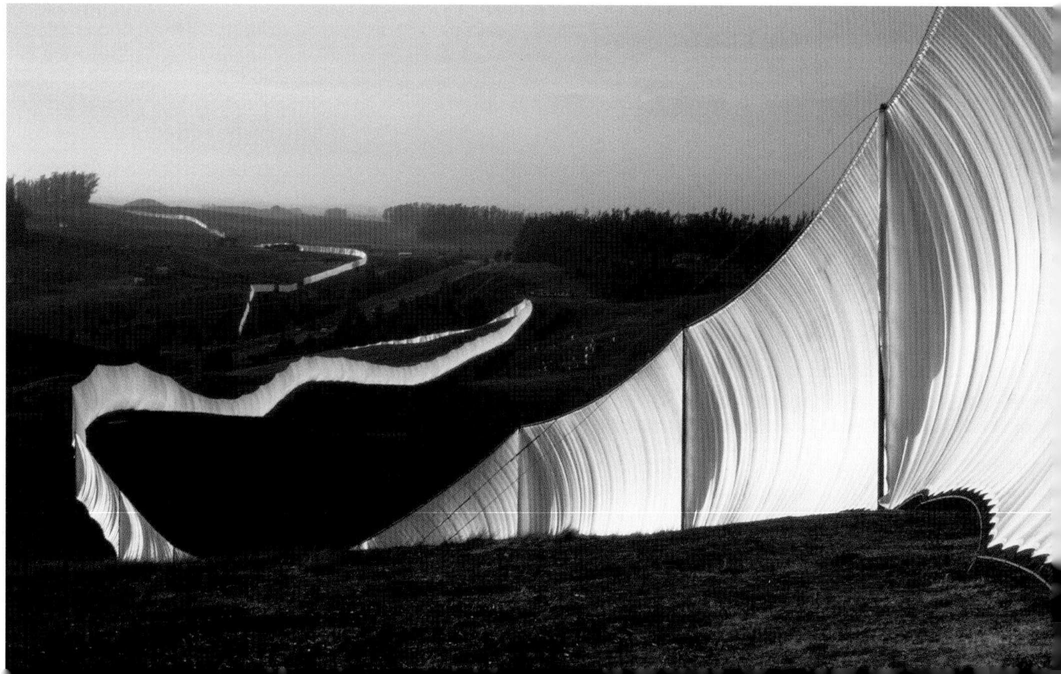

FIGURE 6 Christo and Jeanne-Claude, *Running Fence, Sonoma and Marin Counties California, 1972–76*, 1972–76

mine and yours, in and out, human, plant, and animal. Nothing is more frightening to us than a landscape devoid of difference. No light, no shade; no background, no foreground; no separation of earth and sky, of culture and nature. An undifferentiated landscape is a landscape of fear, tugging the human back into the real of nature. When the landscape loses all its edges, when it becomes pure background without a background, when we think there is nothing behind it, it becomes the grounds of sheer horror: a pool or a pit without a rim or a bottom; a forest without a clearing, edge, or end; a desert without an oasis; a suburb without limits.

Current experimental work calls into question a fundamental opposition in classical landscape design, that between the natural and the artificial. In its 2000 proposal for Downsview Park in Toronto, the design firm Foreign Office argues that the natural and the artificial have become inseparable and indistinguishable. Organic prosthetics, biological computers, genetically modified foods, cloning, and the human genome all emphatically undo the old nature vs. artifice distinction. The new landscape architecture understands that nature and culture have been locked in a life or death struggle. Nature is a cultural category, but not the reverse. And everything cultural was once a part of nature. Can there be room in this town for both of them?

The new landscape architecture is in the vanguard of the movement to accommodate both nature and culture. Nothing impedes progress in this arena more than naive assumptions that it is a relatively simple task, that all we need to do is create more green space. Although this and similar progressive strategies would certanly be helpful, it does nothing to confront the original form of violence that occurred in the seemingly innocent act of naming "nature." Nature quickly departs from the various things we call nature. How much benefit do we derive from a greenbelt that is maintained by massive doses of chemical fertilizer, toxic herbicides and pesticides? Everything we refer to as "nature" or "natural" is now only a symbol or a sign, not so much of nature as of a desire for something we have lost.

A tree planted in a garden is not nature any more than the word "tree" is a tree. The tree in the garden has already left nature and joined the symbolic order. It occupies a privileged place in the garden simply because it is such an effective and beautiful symbol of a lost object of desire—the real of nature. J. B. Jackson once said that vernacular architecture is the result of a confrontation between human aspiration and environmental reality—between desire and the real. In new landscape experimentation, the nature/culture opposition has given way to "constructed nature," "preserved nature," "artificial nature," even "'authentic' nature." The new dialectic is not between nature and culture but between the braiding together of the natural and the artificial on the one side and the real of nature on the other.

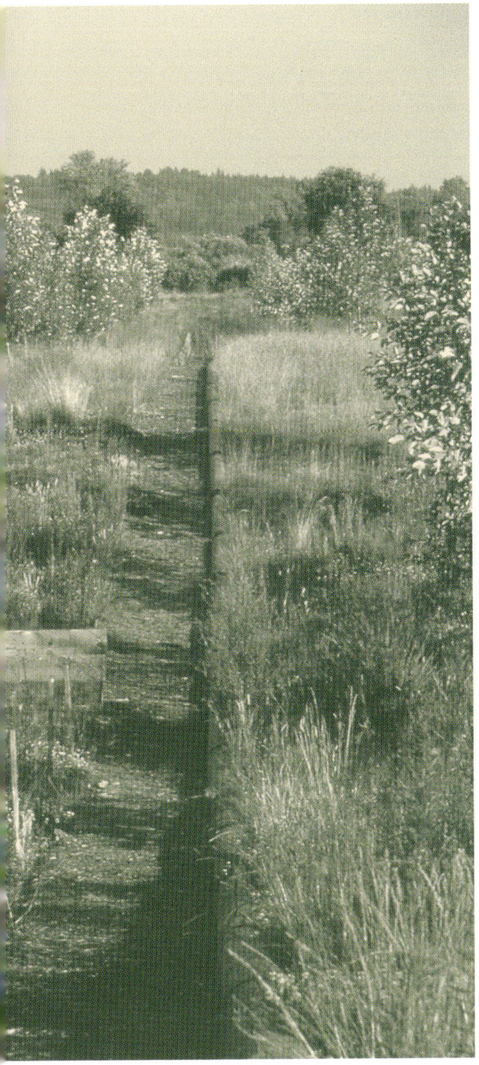

FIGURE 7 Tom Leader for Peter Walker and Partners, *Longacres Park*, Renton, Washington, 1993

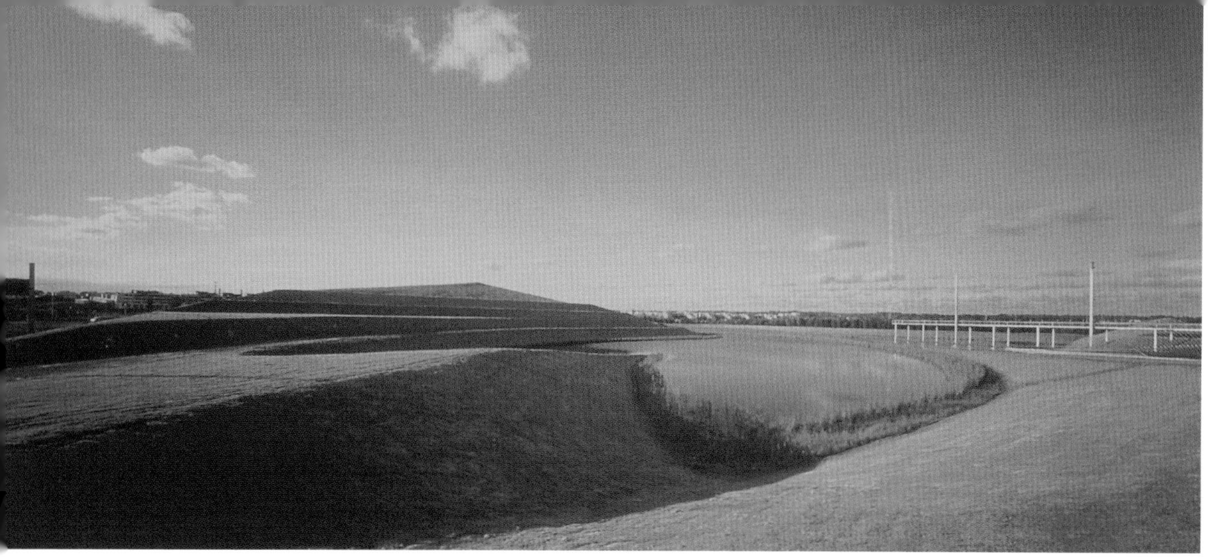

FIGURE 8 Hargreaves Associates, *Sydney Olympic Park*, Sydney, Australia. 1996–2000 Photo by John Gollings

The most interesting recent works in landscape design are self-conciously elaborated around a disappearing nature. Hargreaves Associates created geometric swales at Crissy Field in San Francisco's Presidio and in other projects, notably Candlestick Point Park in San Francisco, Guadalupe River Park in San Jose, and the Sydney Olympics (fig. 8). These angular depressions reference the natural landform that no longer exists while simultaneously referring to the absence of the natural. This is a more complex and interesting strategy than trying to cover up the disappearance of nature with perfect simulacra of natural swales. The geometric swale is a representation of both absent nature and of desire.

At the center of all landscape design is absent nature, a kernel of the real, nature that cannot be symbolized, nature that continues to elude all our efforts to represent it, to construct it, to name it. If nature is not found in the ways we symbolize it, where is it? It is not absent from the world. It is absent only from our cultural productions, especially those that claim to be "about" nature, most especially landscape design. The real of nature is never far away, however. It is all around us and within us. And nature always bats last. Consider the human body. Every microscopic feature of physical appearance is fully inscribed in the symbolic order. Either we do or do not conform to cultural standards that apply to every detail of our appearance. Of course, we paint, dye, trim, clip, curl, exfoliate, reduce, augment, and reshape ourselves to cultural standards. Our bodies are "landscaped." However, just inside our skulls and our skin, hidden from the gaze of the other, is nature. The interior is incorporated into the symbolic as follows: ♥.

This banal symbol has nothing to do with the impossibly real, that is, the heart that pumps or does not pump. Death is real, and death is symbolized. The real of death is what remains untouched by every effort to symbolize it. The same is true of the real of sexuality—the part of sexual experience that can never be contained in cultural or symbolic categories and conventions.

The recent advances in landscape architecture address a new kind of space. It is not merely the space around us but the space that separates the human subject (*Homo symbolicus*) from the impossible lost object of desire. The real. In the case of nature, it is the gap that separates the person from the real of nature that can never be constructed or symbolically represented.

The gap between the person and the real is the space of all design, and of landscape architecture understood in a conventional sense. Throughout its history, landscape architecture has tried to fill this gap with pseudo nature or with cultural artifice. The historic goal has been to close the wound, to heal it with design that either mythifies the possibility of being at one with nature or attempts to subdue nature by making it conform to abstract geometric principles. The idea behind previous design praxis has been to lull us into thinking that we can be either in or out of nature and that our positioning is nonproblematical. This is not revelatory work. It is myth work: as human beings, we can never be *in* or *out* of nature or culture.

The new landscape architecture exposes the ideology and the ethics implicit in the history of design. It addresses the gap between the person and the real of nature in such a way as to credit and acknowledge the impossible. Rather than articulating a pretense that there is no gap, the space between the human and the real is revealed. Something like this sensibility is evident in Kathryn Gustafson's plan to put up a line of Mylar spinners that follows the contours of her San Francisco site for this exhibition (fig. 9). There is no effort to be like nature. The piece is inserted between nature and the experience of wind, calling attention to the separation of nature from experience. It is the spirit of nature, not nature itself, that is mirrored. This is revelatory landscape in a radical sense. By celebrating the gap rather than pretending that it doesn't exist, it opens the possibility that we might attempt to reduce the distance separating ourselves from the real by attempting to get closer to the wind.

Landscape and Place

Landscape architects have tended to think of themselves as "place makers." Increasingly, over the past several decades, controversy over appropriate uses of public and private places has defined civic life. People who have been excluded remind us that place is not necessarily a neutral term, as expressed, for example, in such injunctions as "Whites only," "Stay in your place!" or "Go back to where you came from!"

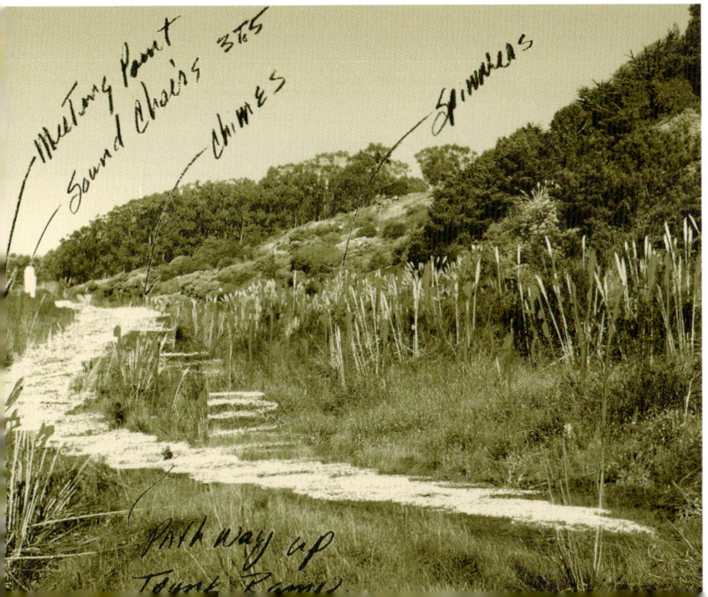

FIGURE 9 Kathryn Gustafson, Jaimi Baer, and Conger Moss Guillard Landscape Architecture, *Wind, Sound, and Movement*, 2001 (site perspective)

Even if a proper and accessible place could be made for every conceivable human type and act, place would remain a problematical concept. The aggregate of places would not converge in a beautiful and functional totality. In fact, what we mainly experience in everyday life are borders, boundaries, and edges where several places clumsily come together. Our everyday experience is fraught with anarchic space—impenetrable barriers, gaps, weird overlaps, and aesthetically awkward juxtapositions. By both necessity and choice, the new landscape architecture addresses those parts of the built environment where previous projects dramatically fail to come together in a coherent fashion. The curatorial statement for the *Revelatory Landscapes* exhibition mentions "derelict and left-over places where we often become most acutely aware of our environment."

This alternative focus calls into question the idea of "landscape as place." It suggests instead that we should be thinking of critical landscape practice in temporal as well as spatial terms as creating opportunities to change places, that is, landscape as the temporal "beyond of place." This has always been true of the landscape, even in its classical mode that pretends to be deployed around a fixed perspective. Landscape needs to be moved into and across in order to be experienced. A landscape is as much a temporal ordering of objects and events as it is a spatial array. Or it can be thought of as a more or less rapid succession of places and experiences, like the different constitutive effects of the men moving through the dark alley. As J. B. Jackson once defined it, landscape architecture is a way to speed up or slow down time.

An alternative way of knowing the landscape and its relationship to place is evident in a Mark Thompson performance piece in which he slowly walked across Japan with a living beehive on his back. The bees go out in search of honey and come back to communicate the location of the honey to the other bees via dance. They are genetically programmed to navigate and communicate, and their program assumes that the hive is stationary. The hive is moving, but doing so in a time structured by their natural limits. The bees can apparently adjust if the hive moves slowly enough. Thompson is meticulously considerate of the needs of the bees, moving very slowly, one step every few seconds. In the video documentation of the piece, it is immediately clear that landscape is the temporal beyond of place. The beautiful Japanese rural landscape moves across the field of vision in "bee time," at about the speed of a lengthening shadow in the late afternoon. The "place" of bees, at once precarious and safely cared for, is revealed in the long shots of the strange man with a hive slow-walking in the distance.

Tom Leader's piece in the *Revelatory Landscapes* exhibition addresses a similar set of issues when the overdetermination of place is a product of culture, not nature. It is located in the corrugated north-south linearity of the Berkeley waterfront. The existing landscape is the product of a chaotic progression of place-making projects that over time got laid down one right next to the others, snaking along the edge of the bay: the railroad, the new landfill shoreline, the freeway, the frontage road, the soundwall. These are all hard lines running close and parallel to one another in a north-south direction. Together they make one of the most naturally beautiful places along the bay dangerous, derelict, and ugly.

Leader calls attention to the series of linear barriers in order to question it and also to suggest alternative east-west traverses. He traces the edges of the freeway, railroad, etc., with low and delicate double fences made of black vinyl screening. Between the two parallel screens he has placed material to serve as a reminder of the geologic and social history of the places destroyed by the monstrous roaring ribbons of concrete and steel. And his fences are interrupted periodically to invite east-to-west and west-to-east movement of people visiting the site. Leader reminds us that even an environment as deterministic as this one cannot overcome the real of nature. Moving east and west, the tides daily gain access to the Berkeley lagoon between the freeway and the railroad. And the fog gently moves from the west across the entire ugly apparatus, rendering it both invisible and dangerous.

This intervention is clearly formulated as the "beyond of place." It should help us to move mentally, and eventually perhaps physically, beyond earlier design disasters. Movement is the key term here. The pieces by Leader and Thompson reinforce the point of the nightscape example previously discussed: the tautological link between human movement and the landscape, that landscape is defined by movement and that the meaning of movement is a function of the landscape.

Landscape and Memory

The design of monuments and memorials in the landscape has not always been exemplary, especially from the standpoint of the memories they supposedly celebrate. Memorials are much more standardized than the memories they mark. Memorializing can become hackneyed. Very often a memorial suppresses memory. On Holocaust memorials, James E. Young comments, "The displacement in memory of one thousand years of Jewish civilization with twelve catastrophic years, is not a happy development."[5]

One of the greatest challenges facing the new landscape architecture is the task of rethinking the memorial. Some of this new thought is evident in the *Revelatory Landscapes* projects. Each of them reminds us that every square inch of ground on which we walk is hallowed, that every inch contains buried memories, that the memorial is not a special type of landscape design project. Every landscape is a memorial. By putting place names in California Indian languages on the supports of a freeway overpass in San Jose, the Hargreaves project reminds us of what we have built on and over, and of the several millennia of gentle occupation that preceded our own. It also reminds us of the weight and overwhelming crudeness of the forces that drove the first Americans from the landscape.

The strongest connection to memorial in the *Revelatory Landscapes* projects is in the fact that all of them will be dismantled. There is no truer marker for the gap between consciousness and a lost object than *absence.* Navajo sand paintings are destroyed in order for the ceremonial process of their creation to be remembered. So long as the painting exists, the act of making it is preserved in it, not in memory. Thus from a Navajo standpoint, the Western process of erecting monuments does not commemorate history but effectively erases it from memory. Perhaps the greatest impact we can hope for from this exhibition of revelatory landscapes is that the brilliance of these alternative works will remain in our memory and influence future design.

5 James E. Young, "Introduction," in *The Art of Memory: Holocaust Memorials in History* (Munich: Prestel Verlag, 1994): 19.

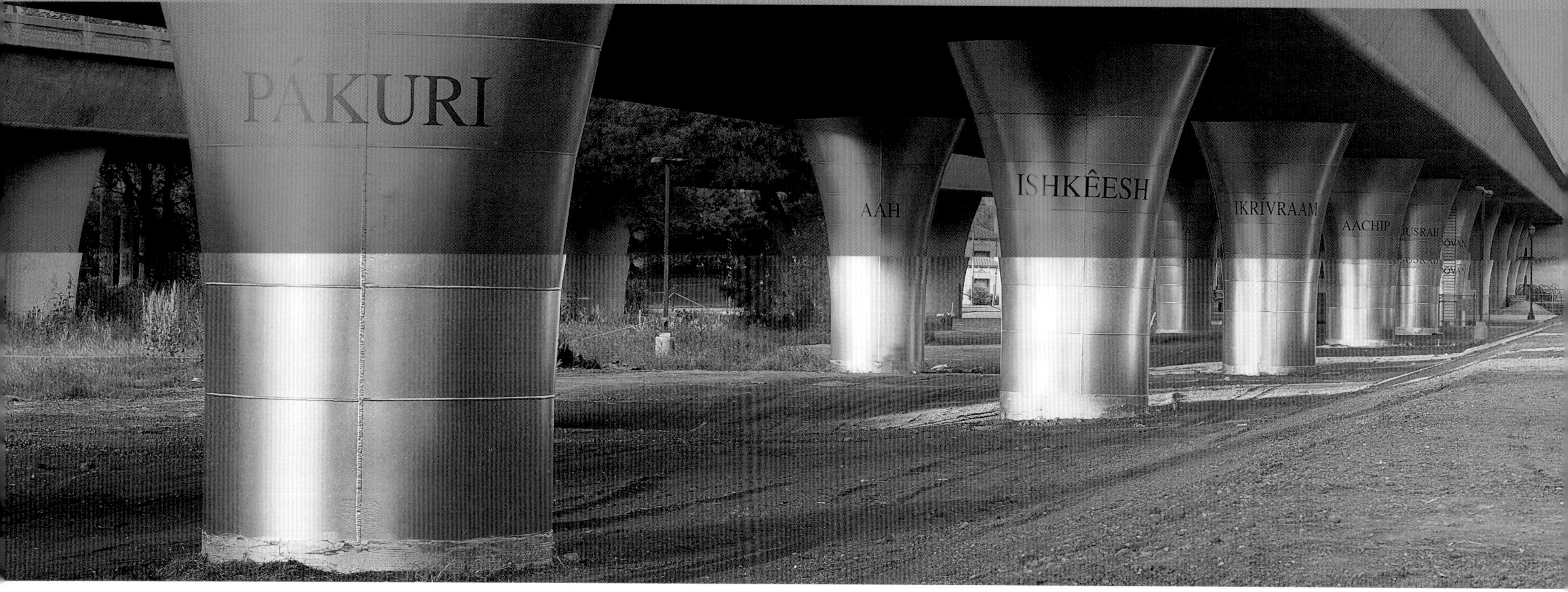
PÁKURI
AAH
ISHKÊESH
IKRÍVRAAM
AACHIP

REVELATORY LANDSCAPES Installations

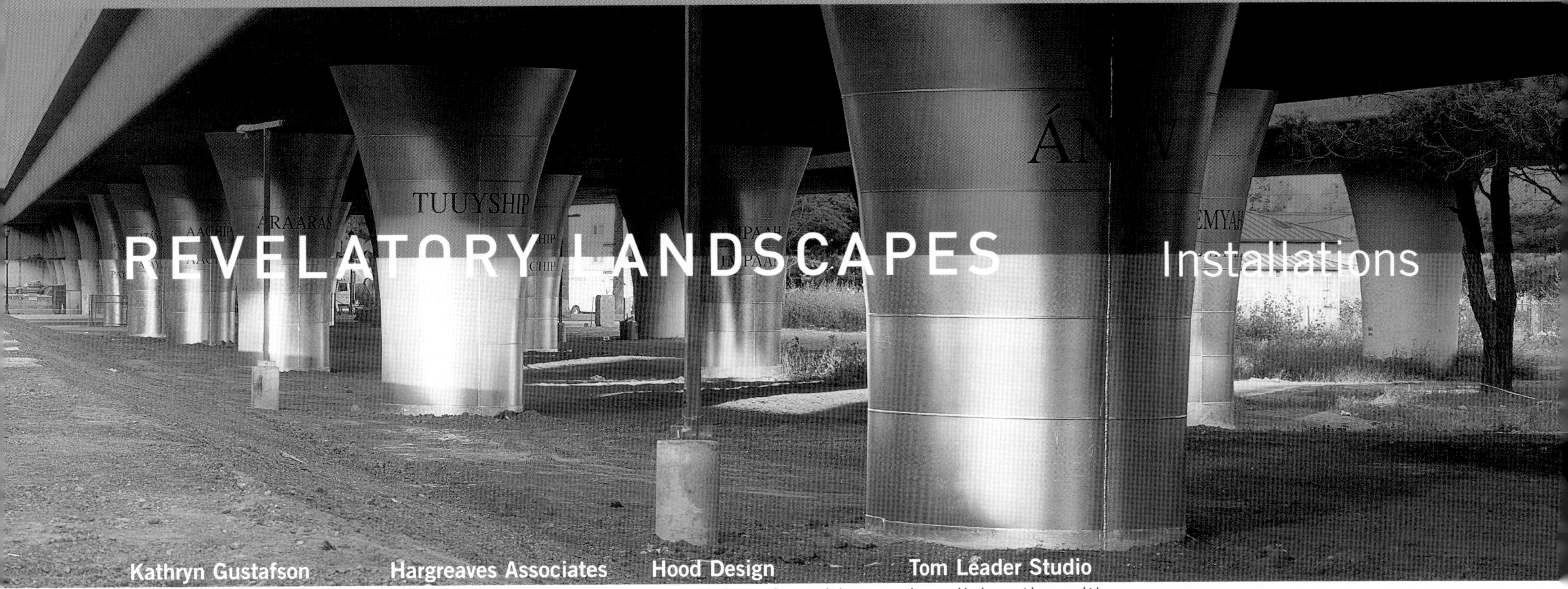

Kathryn Gustafson
Jaimi Baer +
Conger Moss Guillard Landscape Architecture

Hargreaves Associates
in collaboration with
Julian Lang

Hood Design
in collaboration with
Olly Wilson +
Douglas Hollis

Tom Leader Studio
in collaboration with
Anuradha Mathur +
Dilip da Cunha

Text by **Leah Levy**
Photographs by **Richard Barnes**

Wind, Sound, and *Movement*

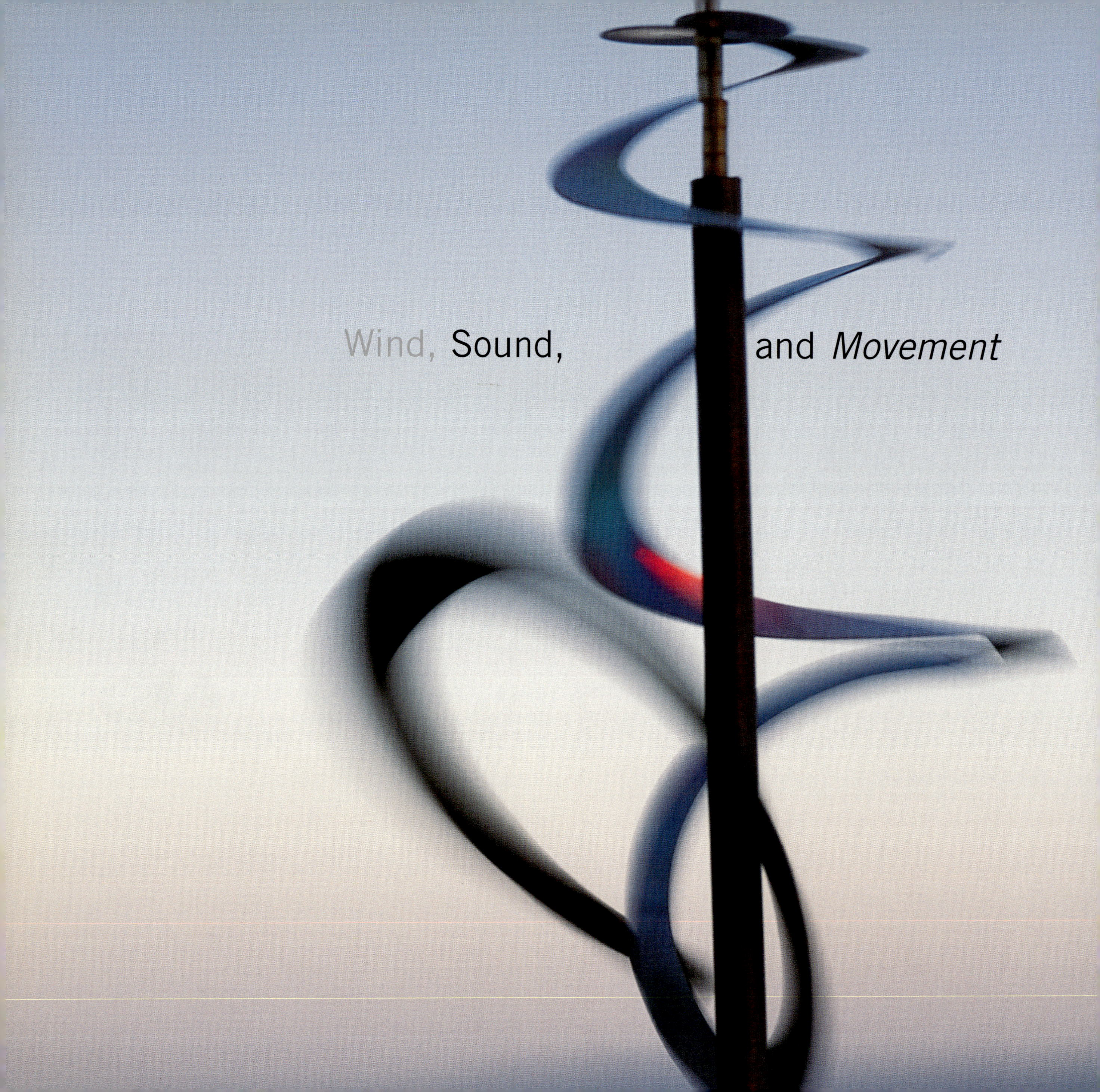

Kathryn Gustafson

Jaimi Baer

Conger Moss Guillard Landscape Architecture

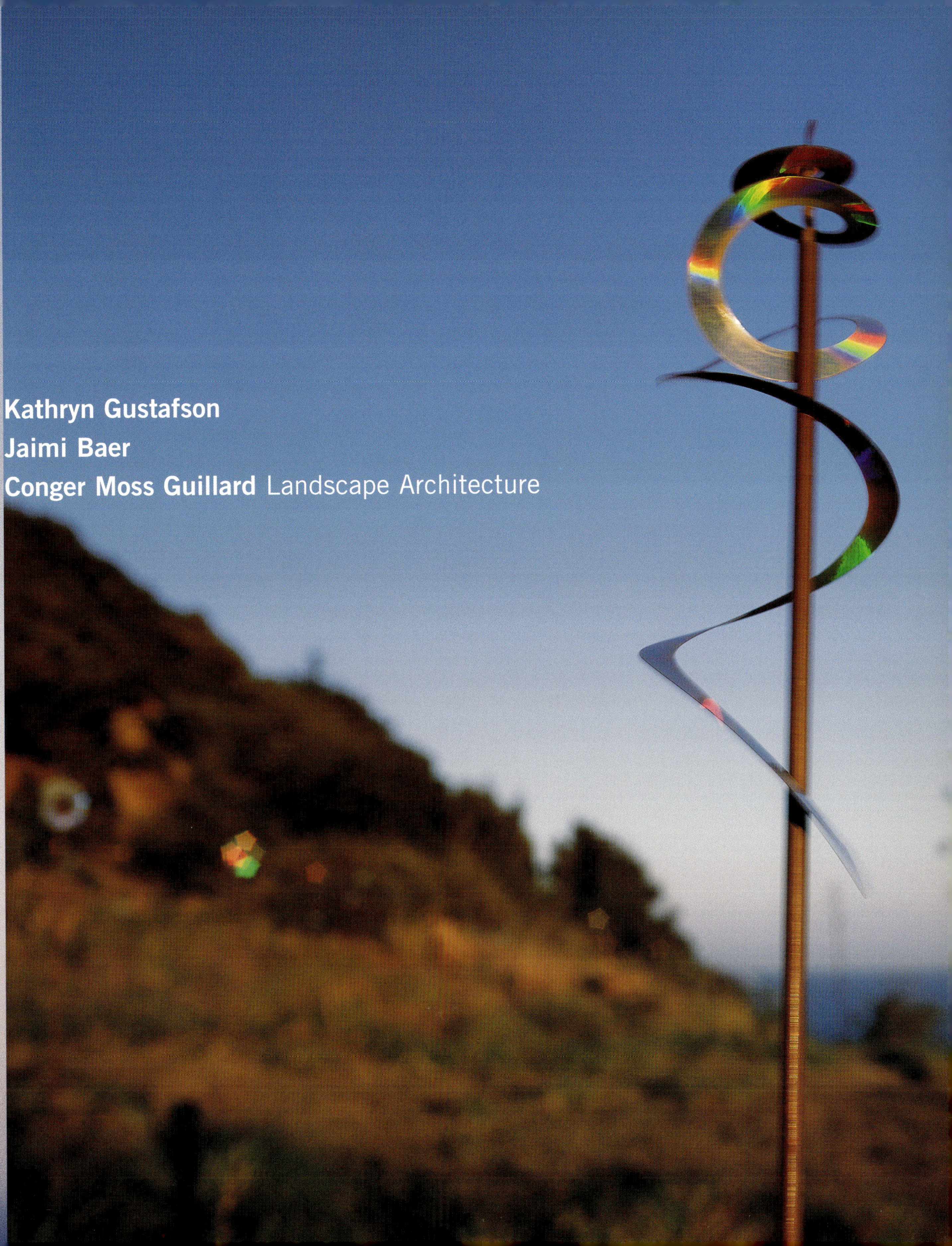

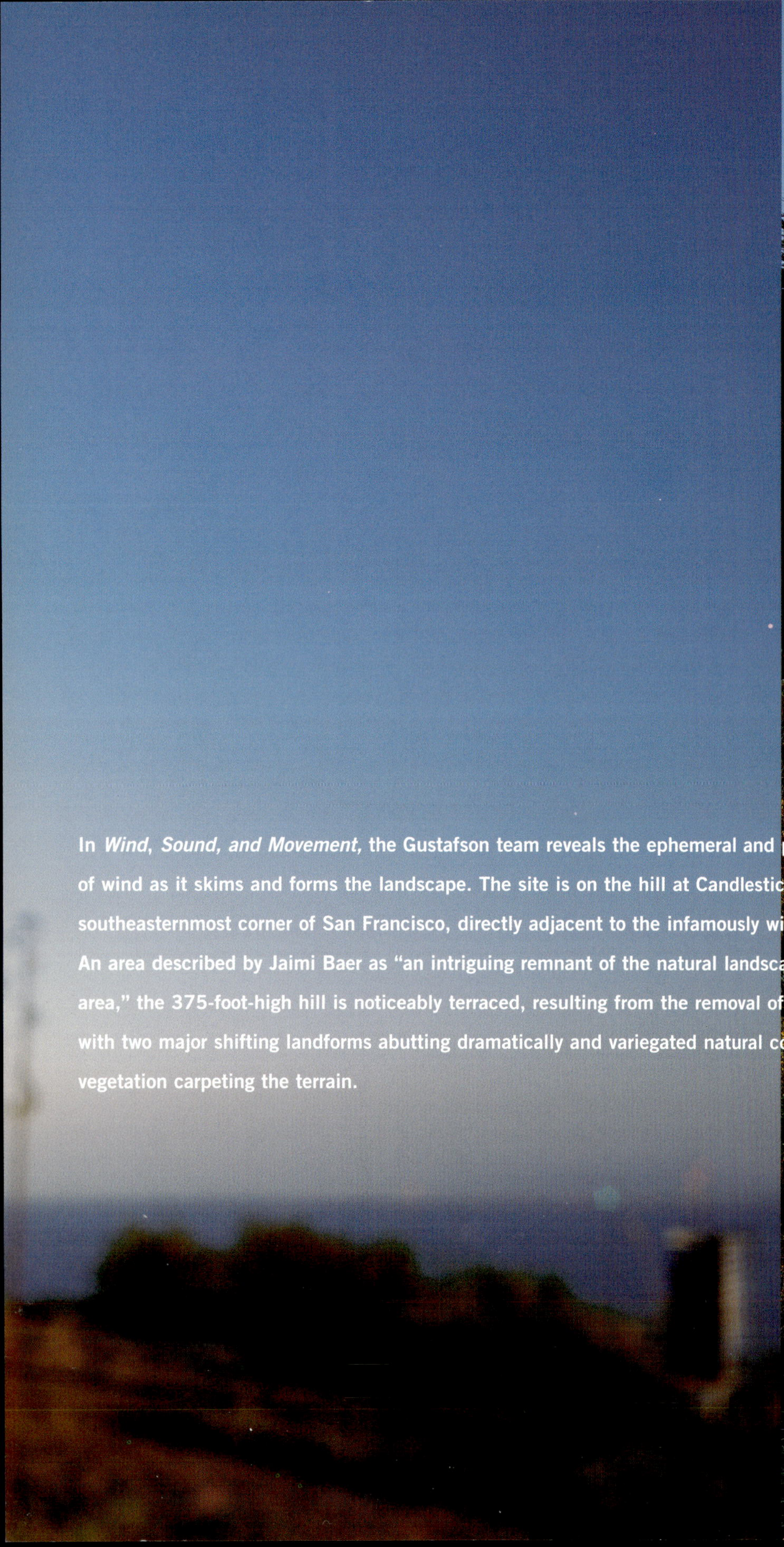

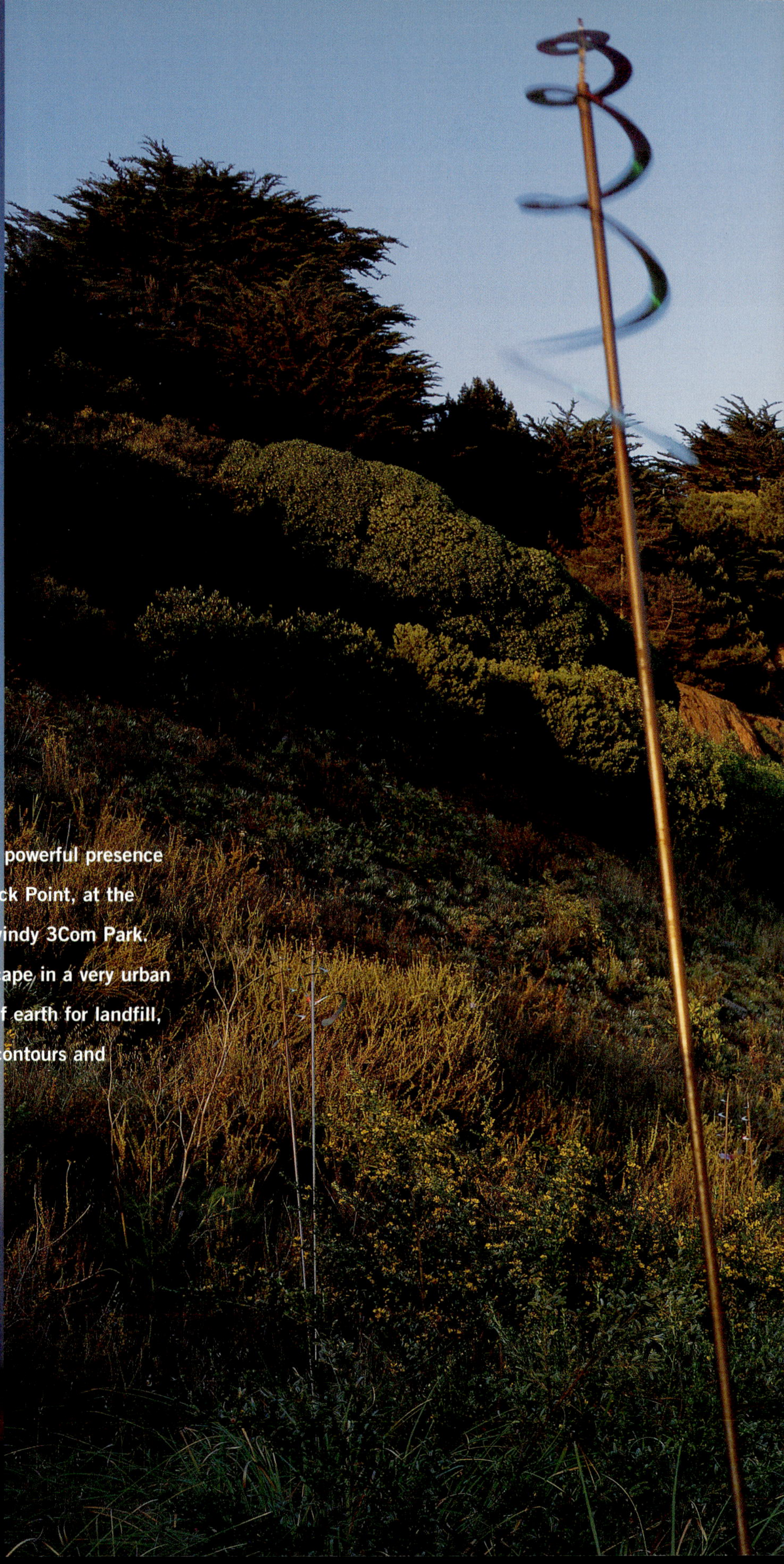

In *Wind, Sound, and Movement,* the Gustafson team reveals the ephemeral and powerful presence of wind as it skims and forms the landscape. The site is on the hill at Candlestick Point, at the southeasternmost corner of San Francisco, directly adjacent to the infamously windy 3Com Park. An area described by Jaimi Baer as "an intriguing remnant of the natural landscape in a very urban area," the 375-foot-high hill is noticeably terraced, resulting from the removal of earth for landfill, with two major shifting landforms abutting dramatically and variegated natural contours and vegetation carpeting the terrain.

The installation exposes the effect of wind—how it shapes what it touches and the sounds it makes and carries while moving across the surface of the landscape. Beginning at the foot of the southeast side of the hill, directly west of the stadium, is an ascending dirt and grass path. After walking several hundred feet, the visitor may hear the faint sound of wind chimes, a kind of aural entry point to the installation. Then custom-designed spiral Mylar spinners mounted on six-foot-high poles appear intermittently along the path. The tall spinners echo the size and shape of the feathery pampas grass, which is plentiful and continues to spring up from seeds dispersed by the wind. Some of the spinners are arranged in groups near clusters of the tall grass; others are woven through the path, gradually increasing in number and opening to a wondrous field of prismatic shimmer. The sun is reflected by the hundreds of rotating spinners, creating an allusive light show, responding to the various velocities of the wind with a magical marking of the site.

Visitors soon arrive at a subtly bowled plateau where the vista of the urban landscape is spread out below, offering the imposing Mount San Bruno, a valley dense with structures, and the ribbon of Highway 101. Sounds are distant but intrusive; the proximity of the highway and the frequent aircraft from the nearby airport generate a significant, if muffled, presence, and the incongruities of the site become progressively obvious.

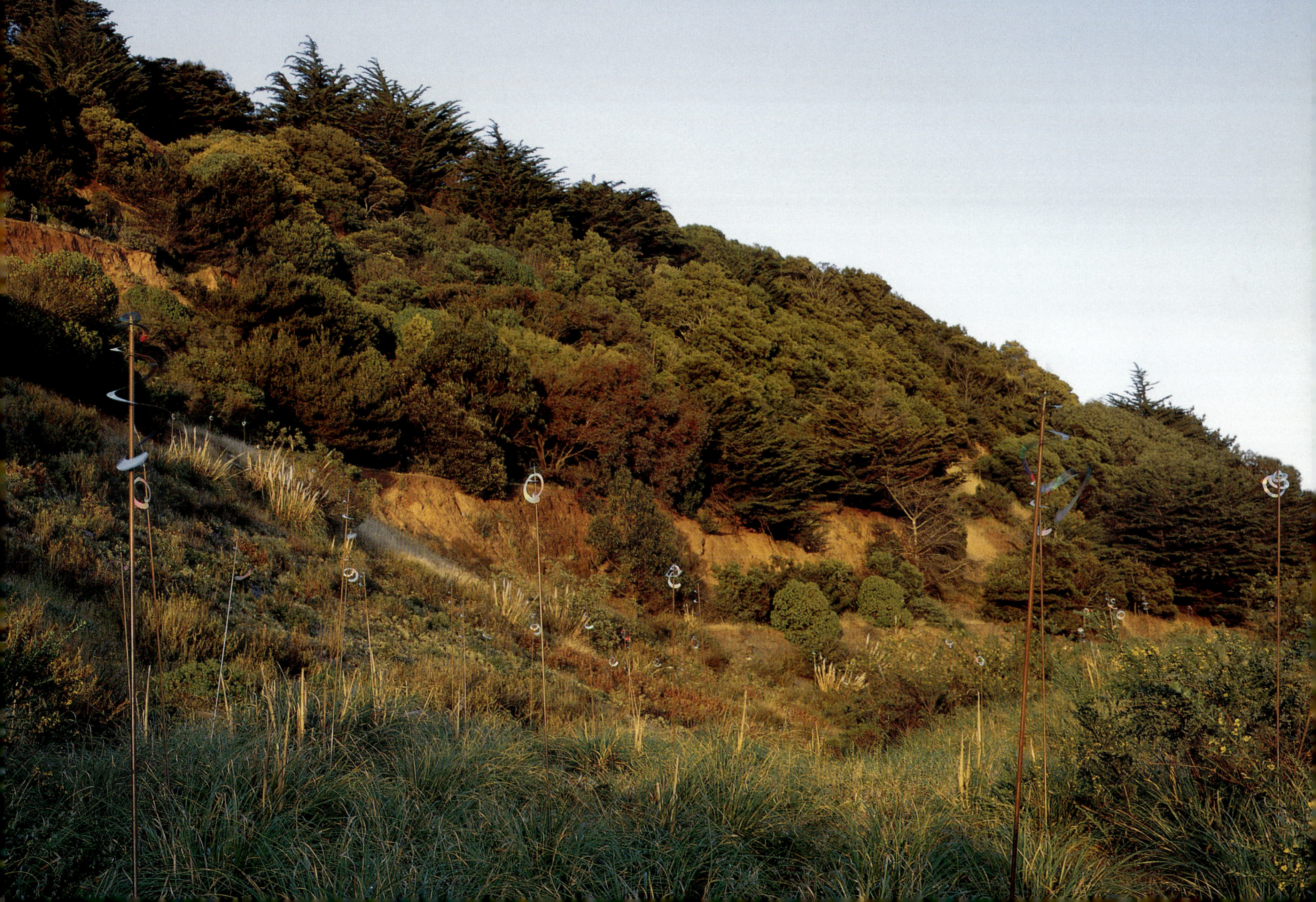

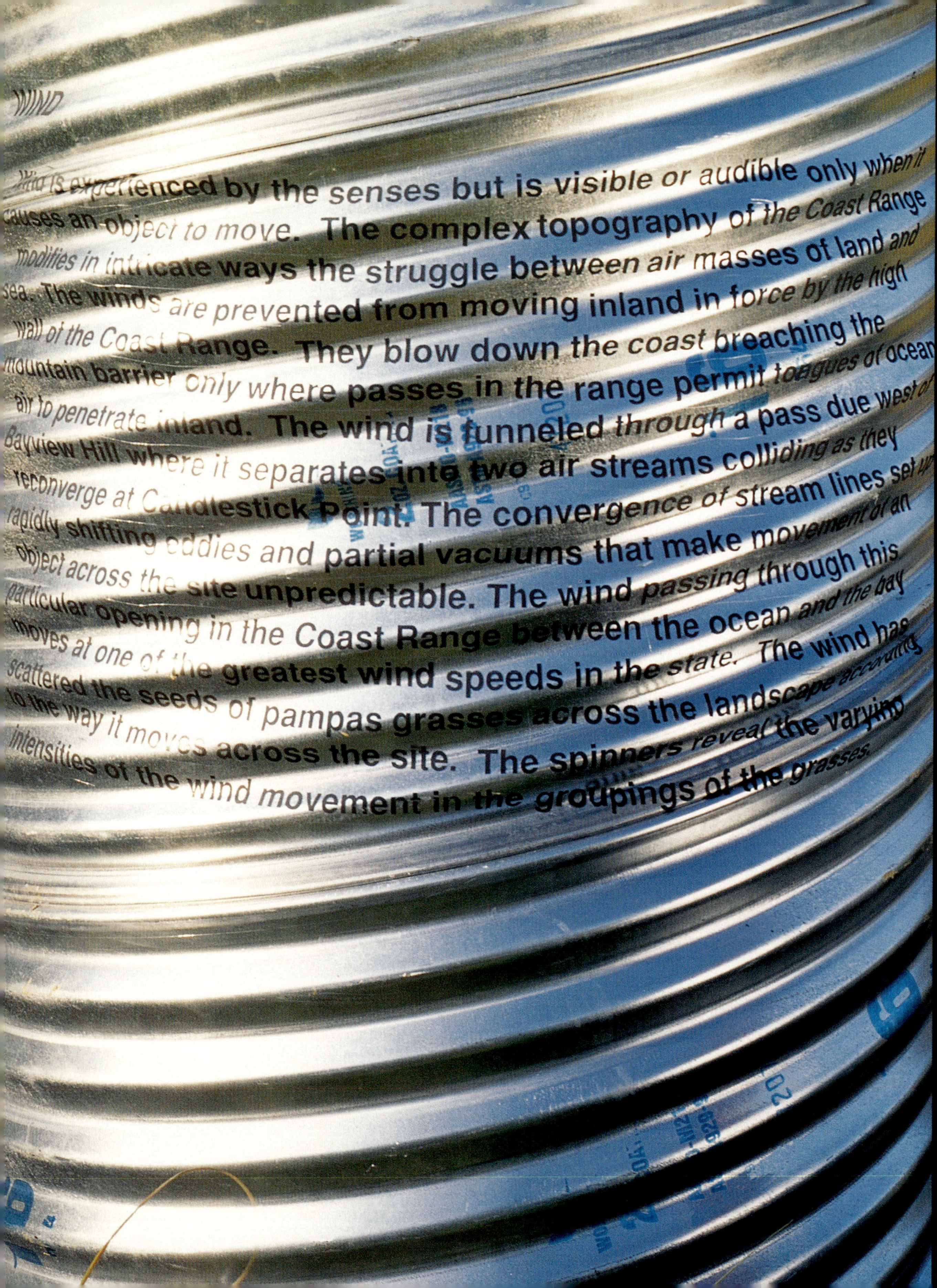
WIND
Wind is experienced by the senses but is visible or audible only when it
causes an object to move. The complex topography of the Coast Range
modifies in intricate ways the struggle between air masses of land and
sea. The winds are prevented from moving inland in force by the high
wall of the Coast Range. They blow down the coast breaching the
mountain barrier only where passes in the range permit tongues of ocean
air to penetrate inland. The wind is funneled through a pass due west of
Bayview Hill where it separates into two air streams colliding as they
reconverge at Candlestick Point. The convergence of stream lines set up
rapidly shifting eddies and partial vacuums that make movement of an
object across the site unpredictable. The wind passing through this
particular opening in the Coast Range between the ocean and the bay
moves at one of the greatest wind speeds in the state. The wind has
scattered the seeds of pampas grasses across the landscape according
to the way it moves across the site. The spinners reveal the varying
intensities of the wind movement in the groupings of the grasses.

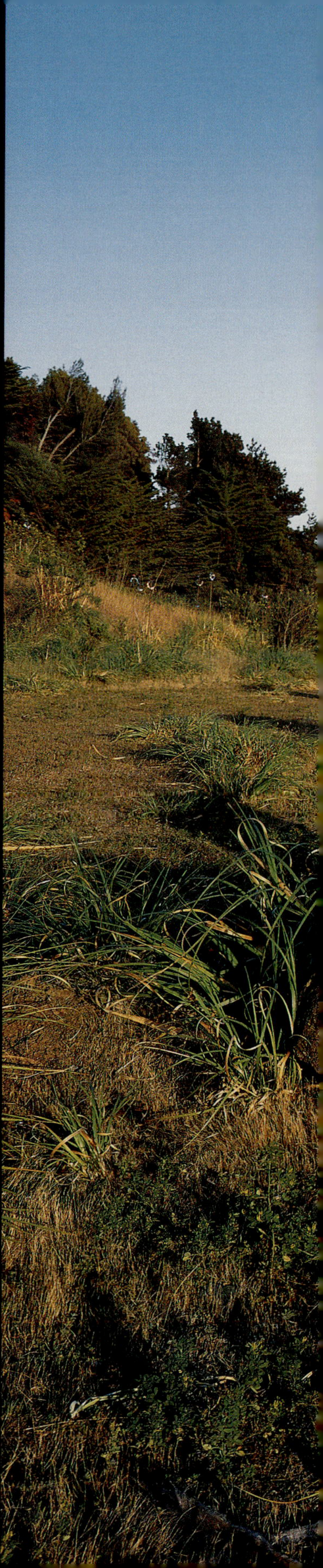

Three "sound chairs," constructed of three-foot-diameter corrugated pipes cut partly in half lengthwise and fitted with wooden seats, are arranged in a row as part of the installation. Sitting in one, with its back blocking the noise of the urban engines to the west, the visitor immediately experiences a different, sequestered zone, one conceived to quiet the environment and emphasize the pleasure of the natural landscape. Birdsongs are interspersed with the rustle of the moving spinners and the pampas grass, providing a delicate and random orchestration for the site. Reinforcing the sense of this unique place, information about the history of the site is stenciled on the backs of the chairs. Those who revisit the installation over the course of the exhibition can track the subtle shifts in the environment over time.

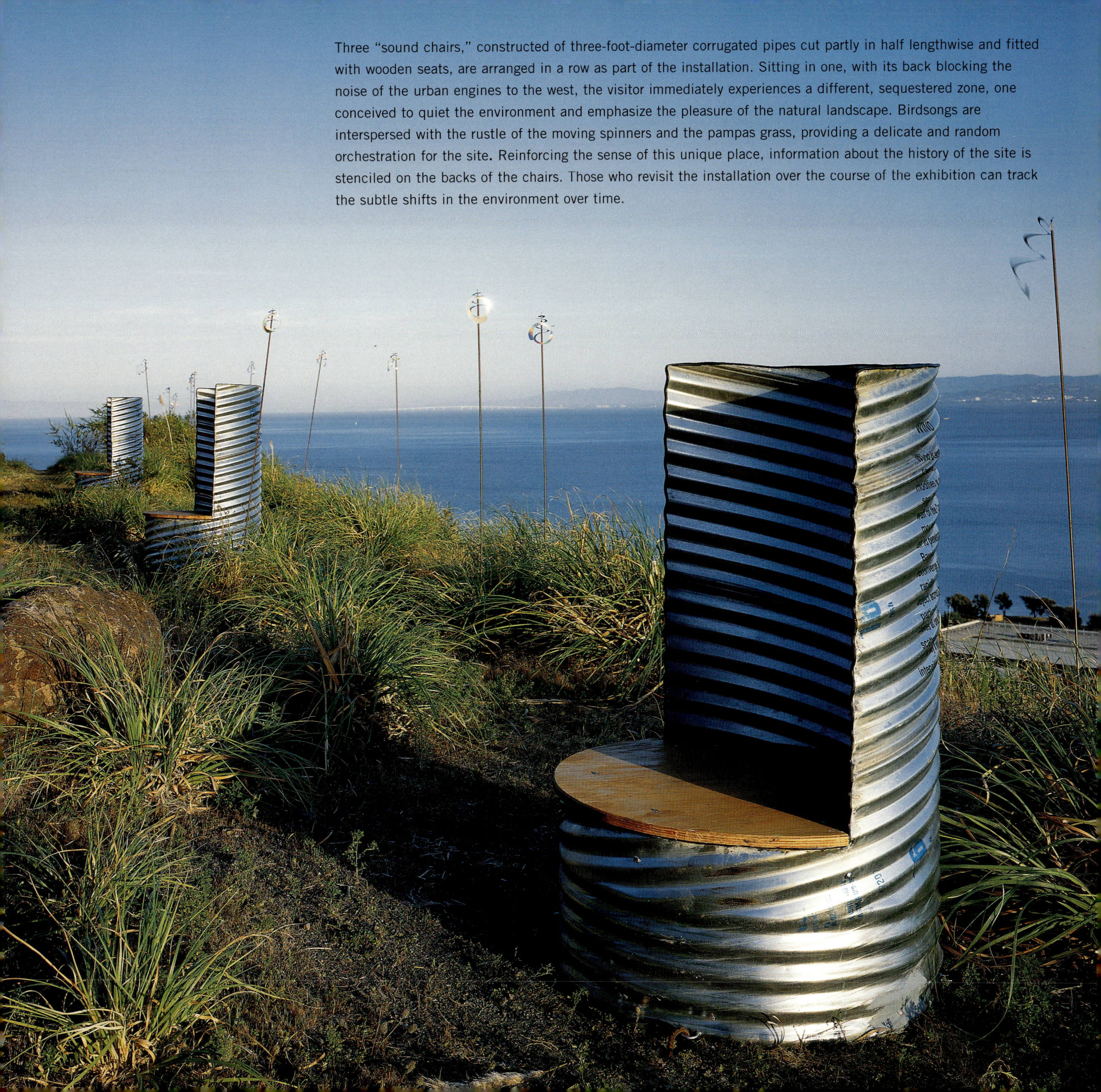

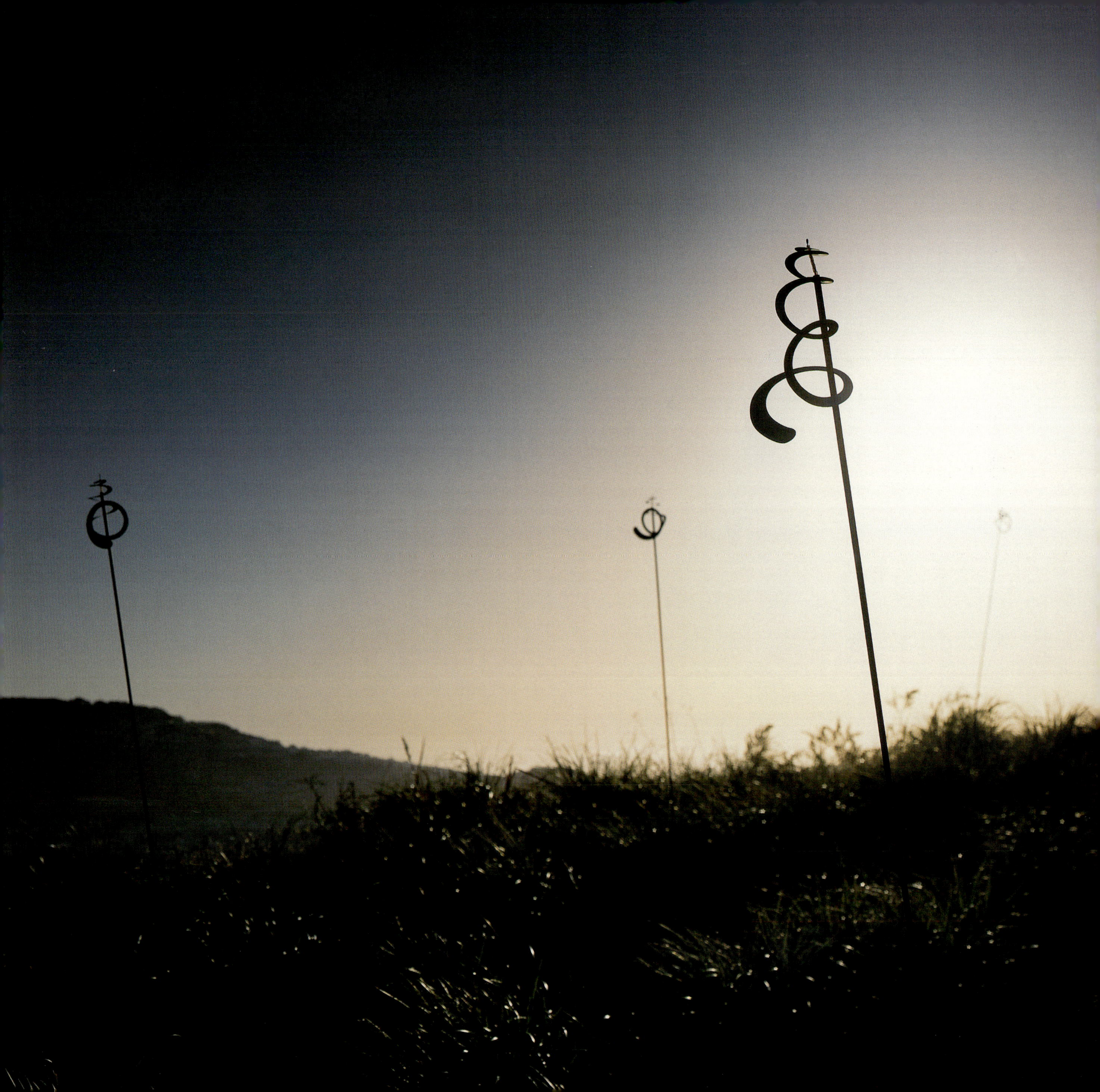

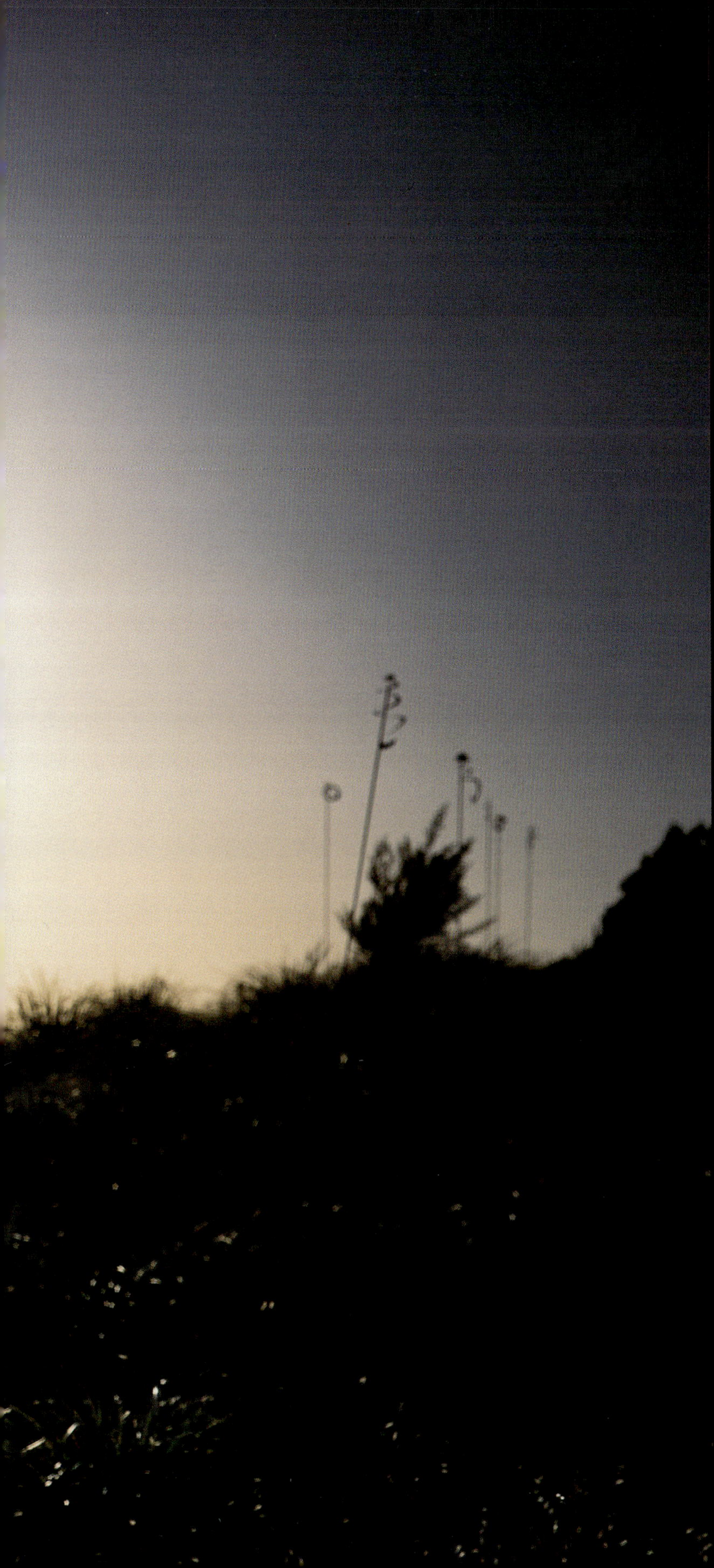

Wind, Sound, and Movement acknowledges wind as an important characteristic of the Bay Area and makes its potency visible. It tracks wind as a force that can be perceived through the environment and captures it for individual encounters and wonder.

MARKINGS

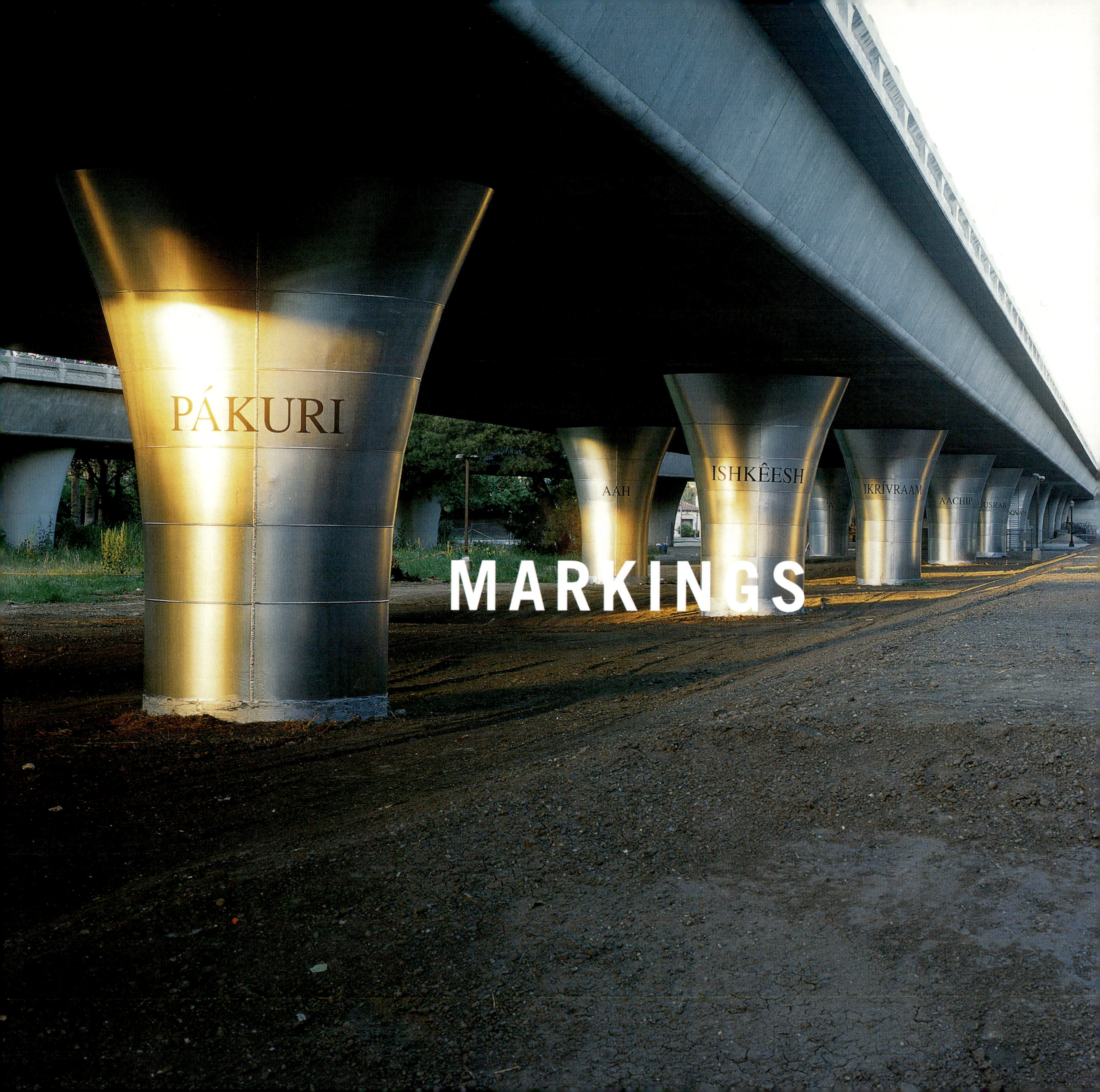

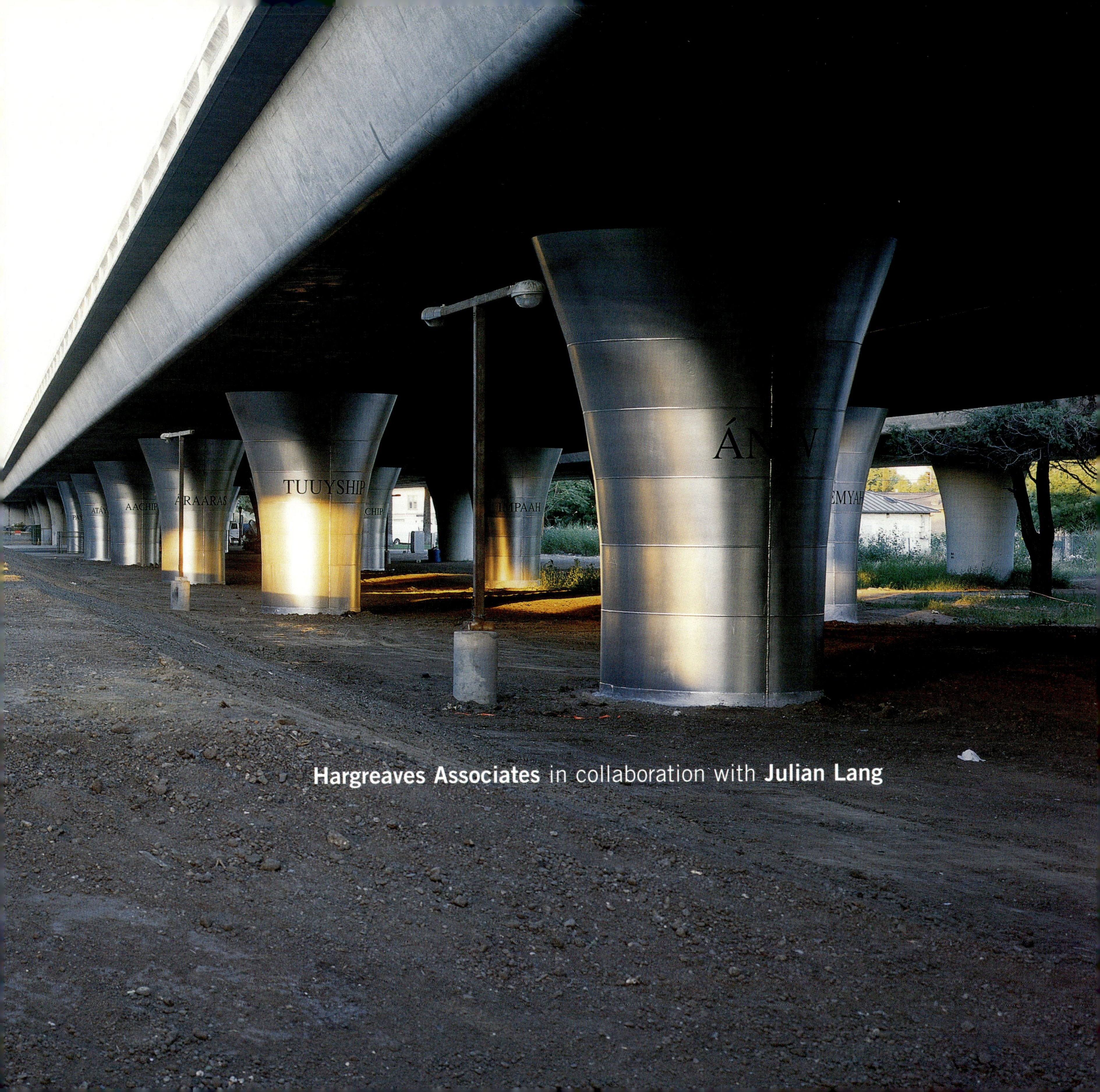

Hargreaves Associates in collaboration with **Julian Lang**

In *Markings*, George Hargreaves and Mary Margaret Jones of Hargreaves Associates collaborated with the Native American linguist and poet Julian Lang to contrast the diverse layers of history and spatial dimension in an almost invisible site, under the interchange of Interstate 280 and Highway 87, adjacent to Almaden Boulevard in San Jose. The four-acre space in the middle of the developed city is a complex one, a collision of nature, massive infrastructure, and evolving cultures. Once inhabited by the Chocheño people of the Costanoan tribal group, whose culture was integrally tied to the nearby Guadalupe River, the area has been primarily populated by a Latino community for the past two centuries. More recently, an expanding new culture, generated by the burgeoning high-tech industry, has joined the locality.

As one arrives at the site, a new physical and visual field becomes apparent. The installation space is an enveloped environment, strangely calm despite its location underneath the freeway. It is occupied by a grid of giant concrete pylons, fifteen feet high by seven feet wide, which support the massive freeway above. These are aligned in diminishing perspective with the Guadalupe River, which lies just out of view at the vanishing point of the field. Twenty-four pylons are sheathed with a shiny aluminum paint, adding a dramatic luminosity and beauty to their forms. Each is carefully marked in black paint with words suggesting sacred intent. On the side of the columns visible at the entrance to the site from Almaden Boulevard, single English words present a simple, poetic evocation (path, mountain, forever, song). Only when one has walked to the far end of the site and has turned to retrace one's steps are the native words revealed on the other side of the pylons. These are the indigenous counterpoints to the English words. They express a belief in myth as a conveyer of truth, and in an essential connectedness between humans and the earth.

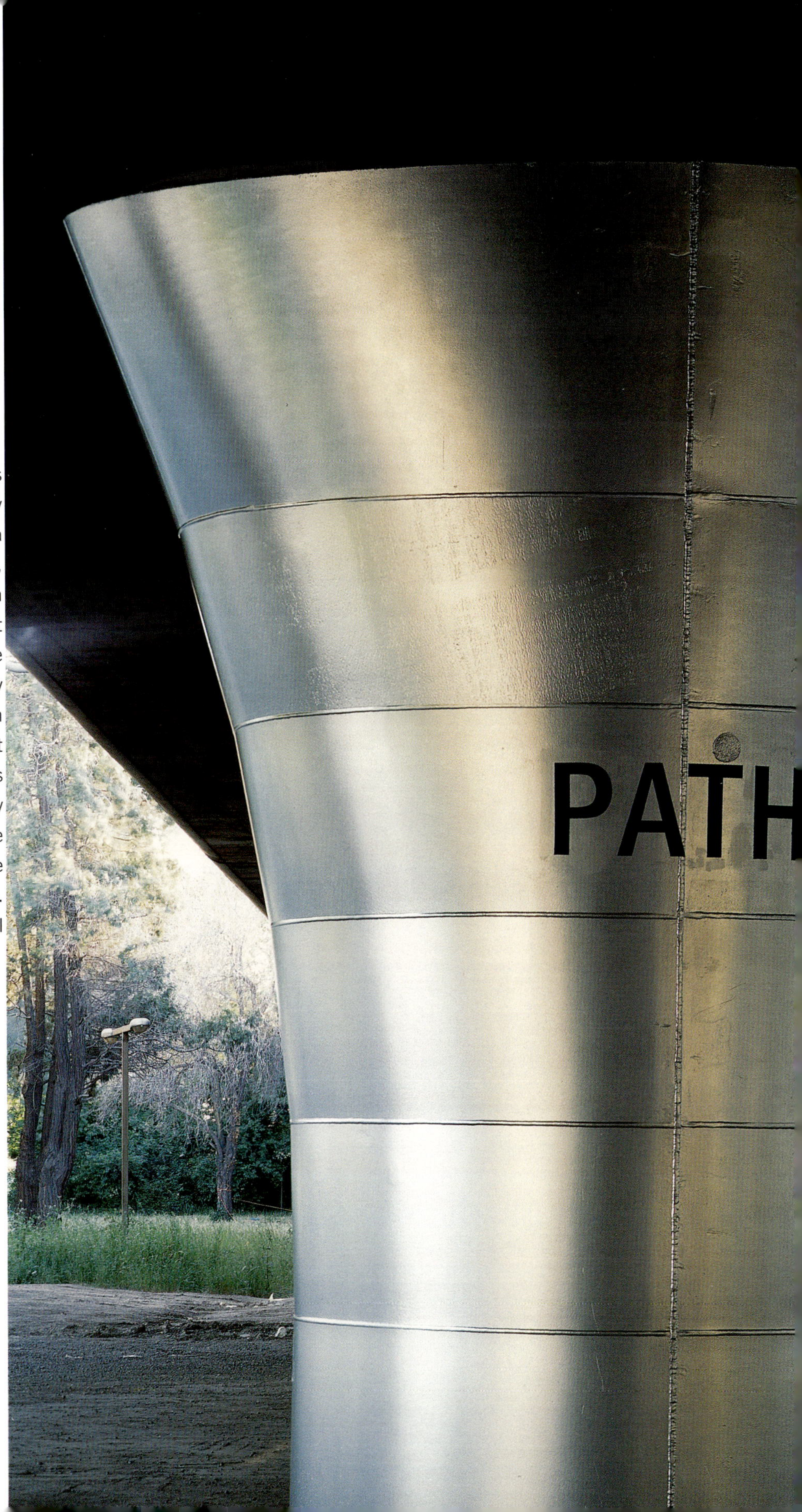

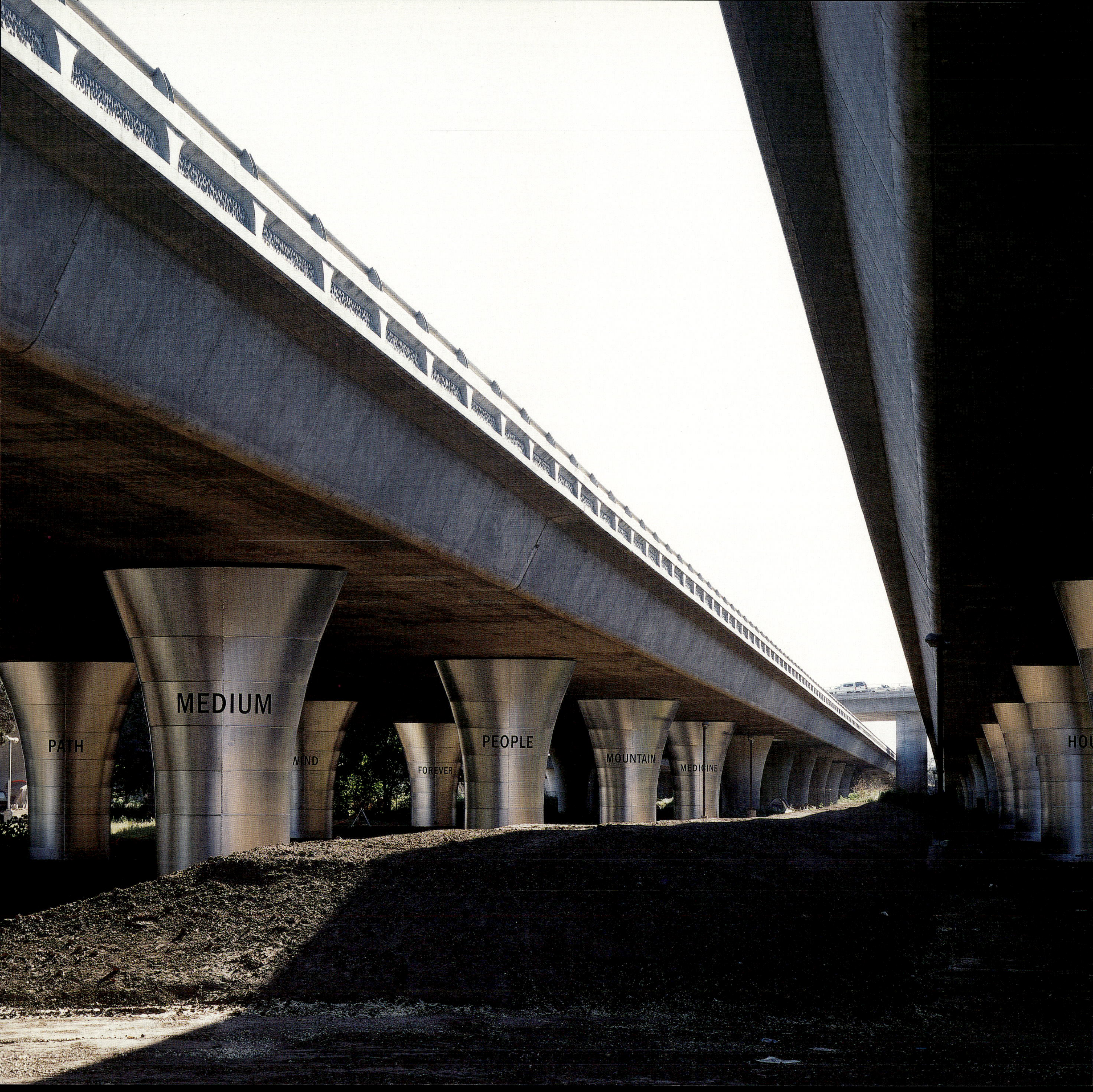
MEDIUM
PATH
WIND
FOREVER
PEOPLE
MOUNTAIN
MEDICINE

In the center of the space stands an earth form, twenty-four feet wide and four feet high, created from fourteen hundred cubic yards of imported soil. Extending for four hundred forty feet, the berm further defines the site as it repeats in shape (and metaphorically fills in) the gap between the road decks above. Serving as both a raised walkway and a form to be walked around and explored, the mound is clearly man-made and yet holds intimations of the ancients: an ascension, a suggestion of a burial mound, a mysterious and inexplicable construction. The sky, always there and usually ignored, is suddenly presented anew.

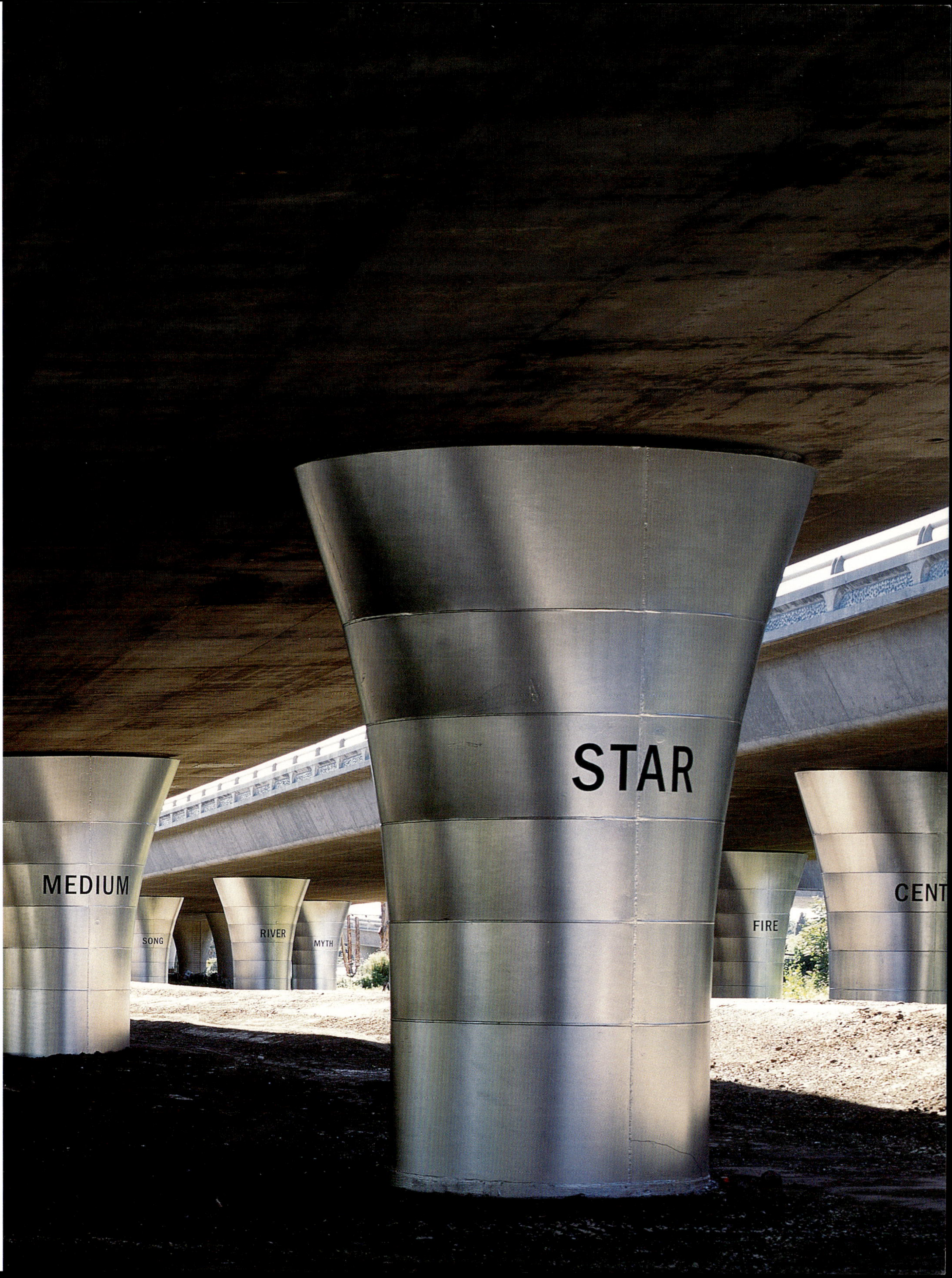

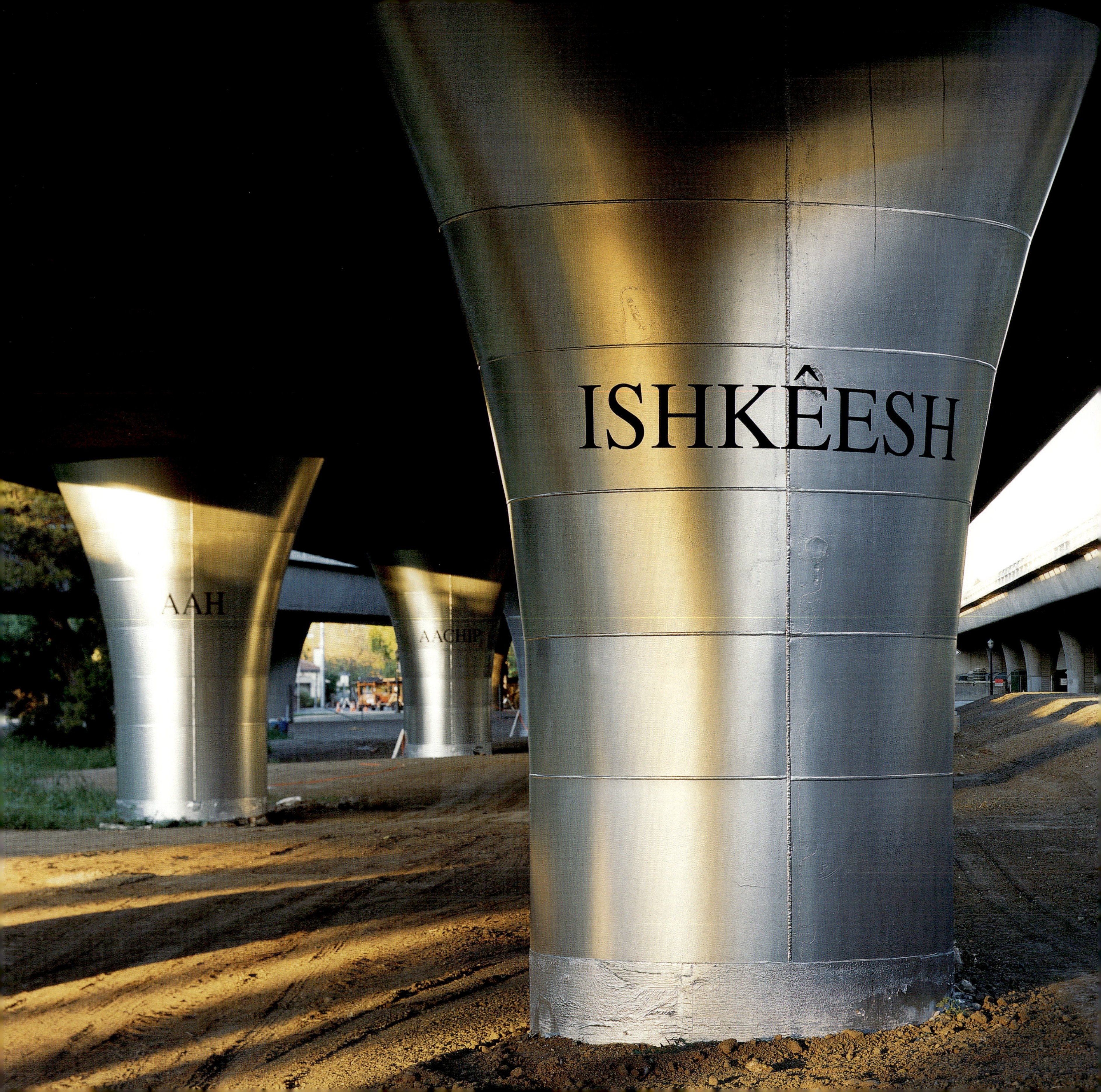
ISHKÊESH
AAH
AACHIP

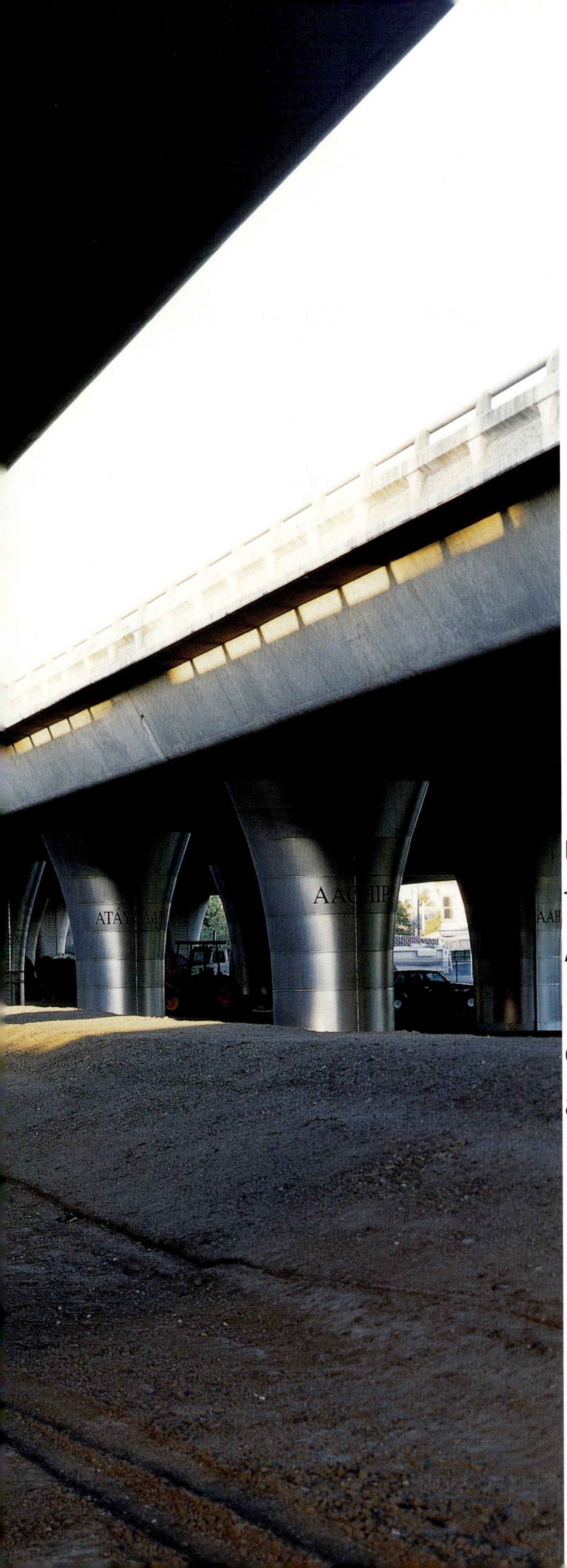

Markings encourages the visitor to "walk the land," as a farmer might pace out cultivated fields, moving toward and through the simultaneously ancient and futuristic concrete forest. Attempting to find one's right size and place in this setting is like focusing a lens. The confluence of magnified and diminished scale, the roaring sound from the freeway overhead, and the rawness of the earth create a surreal yet familiar and memorable landscape.

In *Landscape in Blue—Entropy in the Landscape*, Walter Hood exposes three blocks of what he refers to as "succession landscapes" on Seventh Street in West Oakland. By evoking the entropic dissolution of the neighborhood, the installation reveals the history of the physical and social landscape of the site. These blocks are remembered as a nexus of African American community and creativity during their jazz heyday in the 1930s and mid-1940s, when Slim Jenkins's club hosted such celebrated musicians as Earl "Fatha" Hines, Thomas "Fats" Waller, and the Ink Spots.

Landscape in Blue

ENTROPY IN THE LANDSCAPE

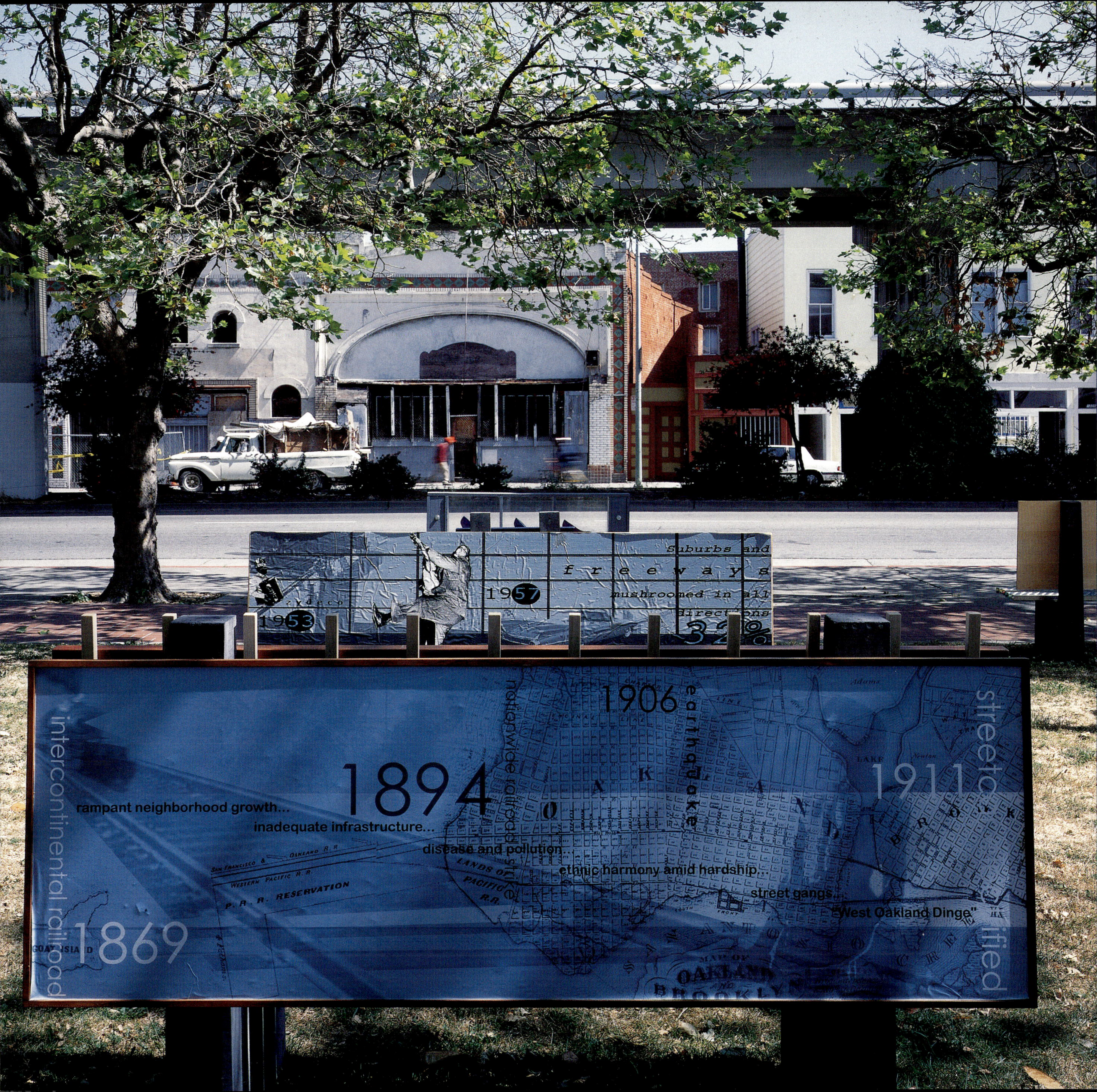
Suburbs and
freeways
mushroomed in all
directions
1953
1957
intercontinental railroad
1869
1894
rampant neighborhood growth...
inadequate infrastructure...
disease and pollution...
ethnic harmony amid hardship...
street gangs...
"West Oakland Dinge"
nationwide railroad strike
1906
earthquake
1911
P. R. R. RESERVATION
WESTERN PACIFIC R.R.
OAKLAND

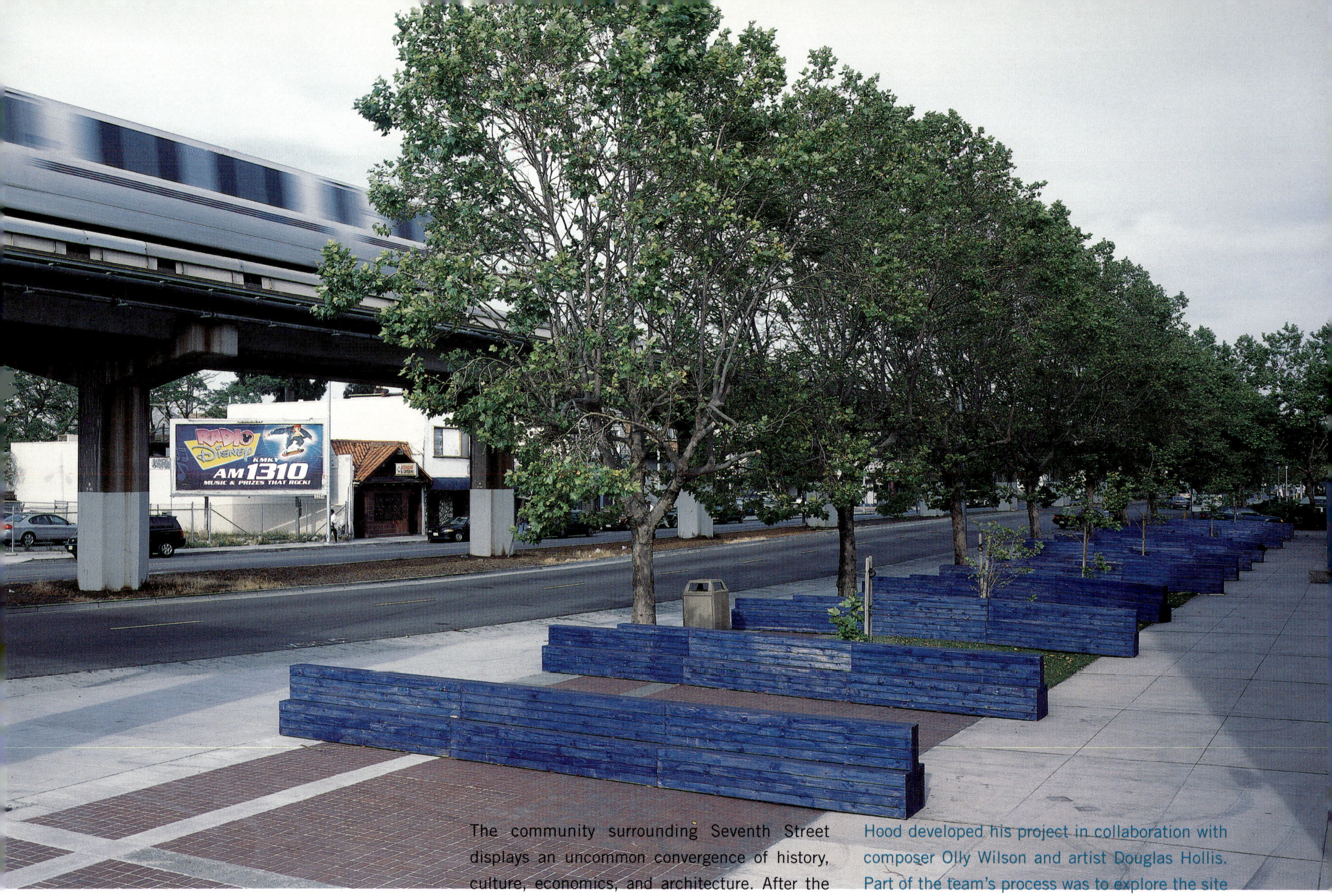

The community surrounding Seventh Street displays an uncommon convergence of history, culture, economics, and architecture. After the advent of redevelopment in 1949, the corridor became the eventual repository of the massive hulks of the U.S. Postal Processing and Distribution Plant and the West Oakland BART station and elevated tracks. Despite the jobs and transportation they provided for the community, they created a fractured domain that remains to this day. The landscape comprises vestiges of an early community of single-family dwellings, mixtures of both new and older housing with light industry, extensive redevelopment, and the nearby bustling Port of Oakland.

Hood developed his project in collaboration with composer Olly Wilson and artist Douglas Hollis. Part of the team's process was to explore the site by means of a variety of musical improvisations. The multifaceted installation was inspired by a twelve-bar blues form, the same rhythm that once brought vitality and a sense of place to the site. The sheer volume of the BART trains intermittently screeching and rumbling on the elevated tracks becomes an ironic balance to the memory of blues and jazz. Large sheets of reflective aluminum hang from the north side of twelve of the hexagonal pylons that support the BART tracks. This creates a kind of proscenium, vibrating as the BART trains roll overhead and the wind from moving vehicles blows through. The old buildings on the north side of the street are reflected on the mirrored pylons, creating the illusion of the space of a previous time.

At the corner of Seventh and Peralta Streets, Hood (still referencing the twelve-bar rhythm) marks the site of a former church, using four rows of six benches made specifically for the project. Each offers its own interpretation of the neighborhood, some displaying texts and images detailing aspects of the site's history. As a group, they provide a gathering place, reminiscent of the site's previous function. On the lawn to the west of the main postal building are twelve low wooden walls, painted an intense blue. Each is stenciled with the address of the building that was torn down to make way for the postal parking structure now occupying the space. The position of the walls replicates the foundations of the single-family dwellings that once stood here on small individual lots. This is currently the site where municipal buses pull up, lunchtime food trucks arrive, and smokers congregate—the last place for social interaction on this part of Seventh Street.

Landscape in Blue—Entropy in the Landscape frames the palimpsest of the corridor, its great musical years and the monumental construction that followed after the "Oakland Blues" lapsed. Only Esther's Orbit Room remains, the last remnant of that rich time, isolated and miniaturized in the environment. By reviewing the world-class, community-generated music and its cultural icons, displaced by the imposed structures, the installation exposes the reality and magnitude of our loss.

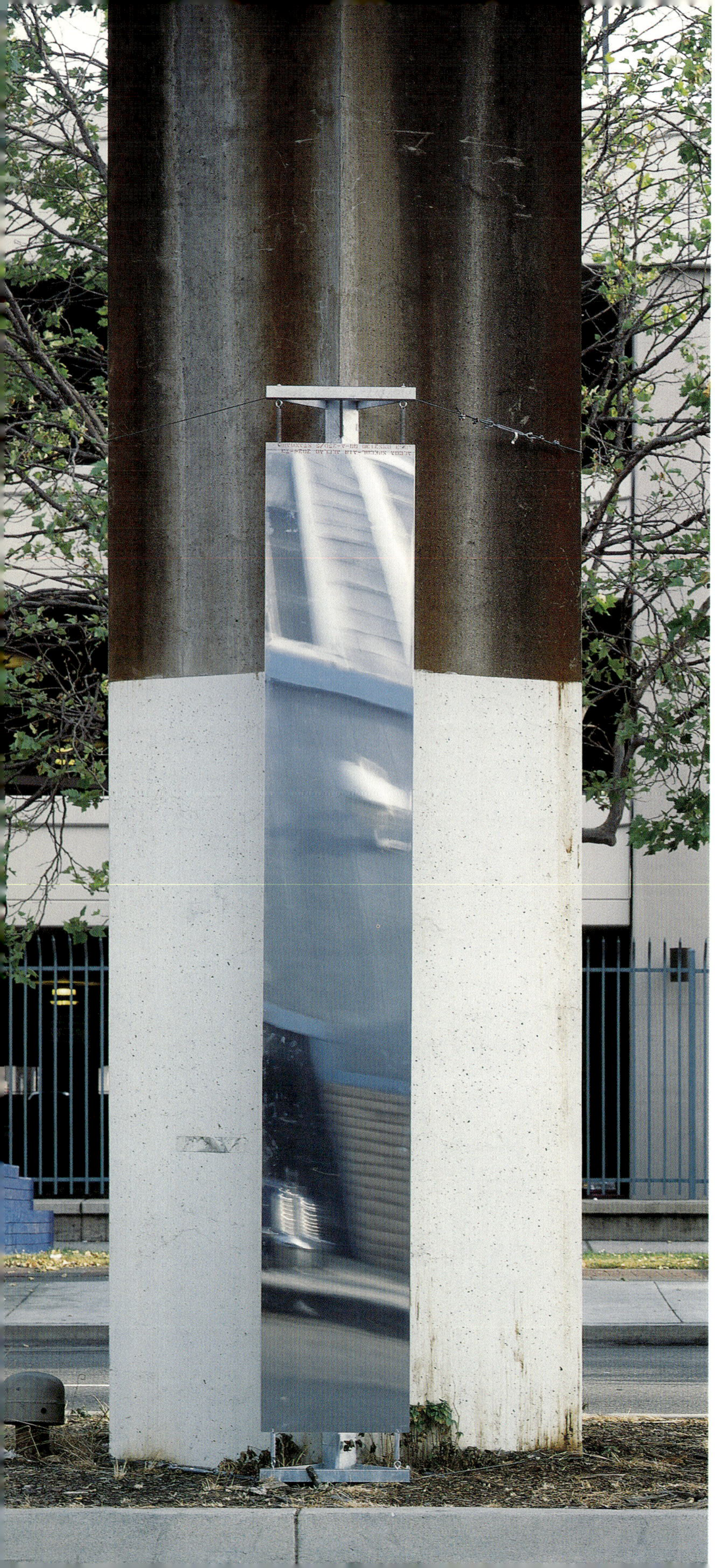

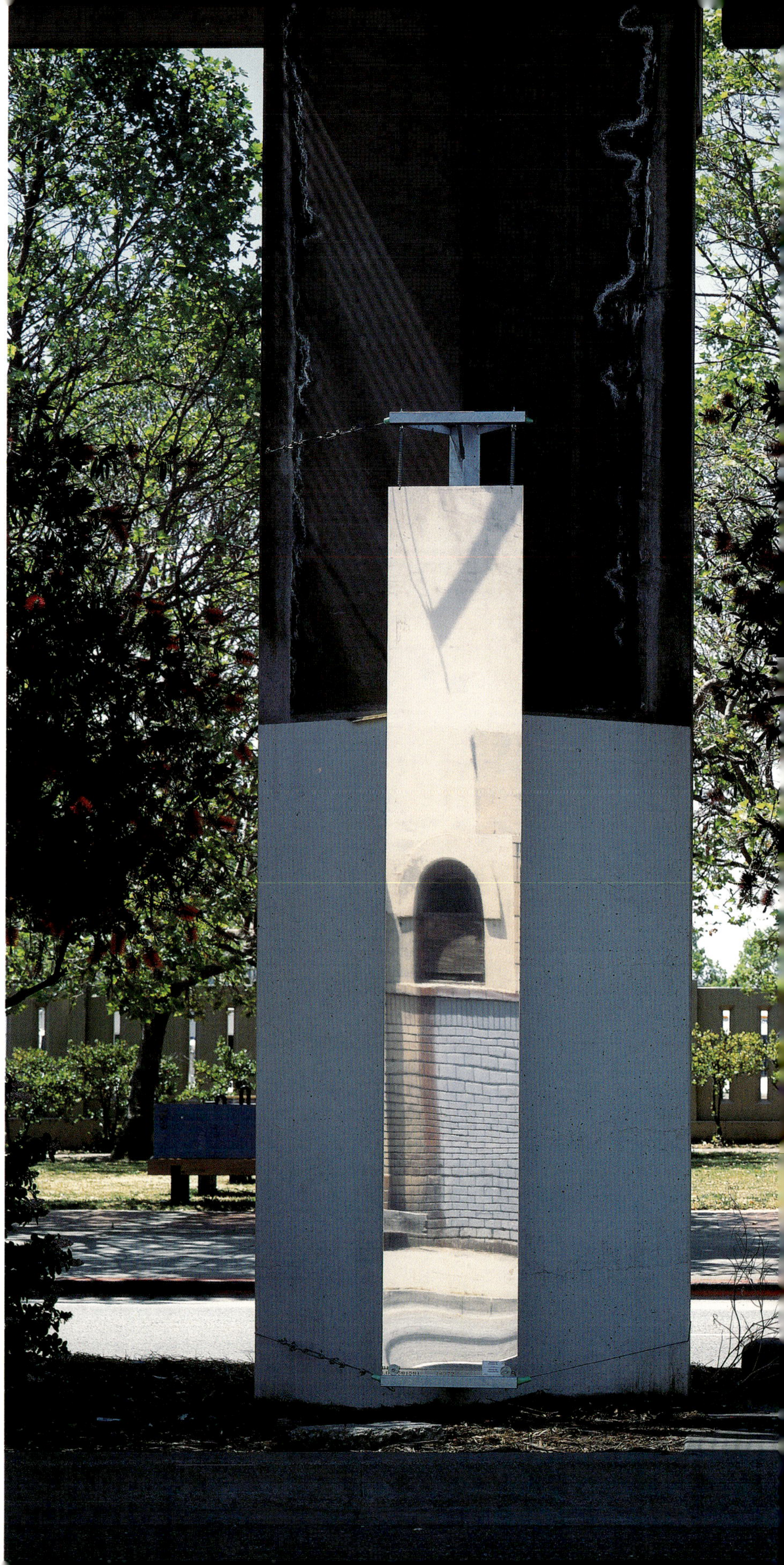

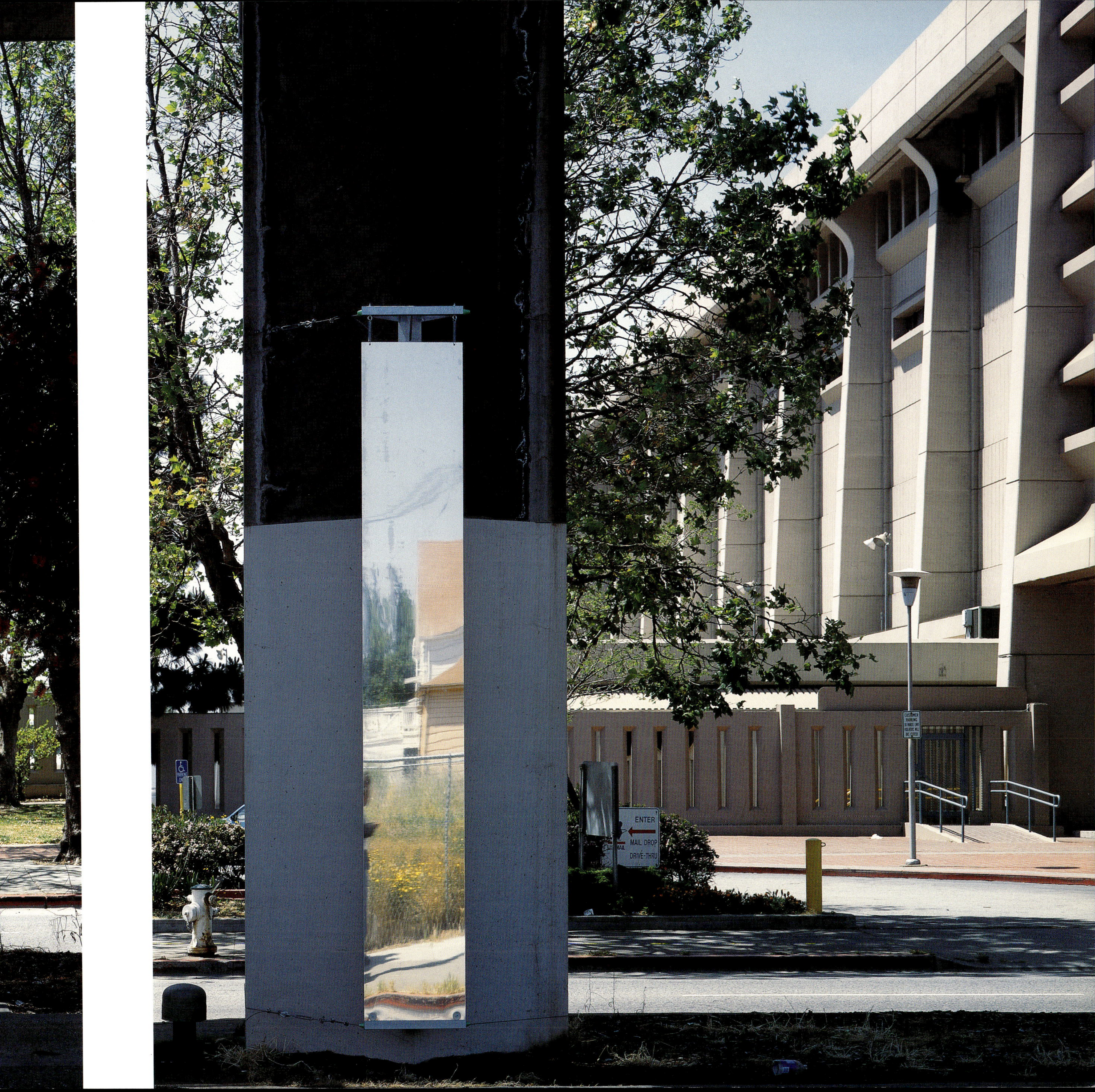
ENTER
MAIL DROP
DRIVE-THRU

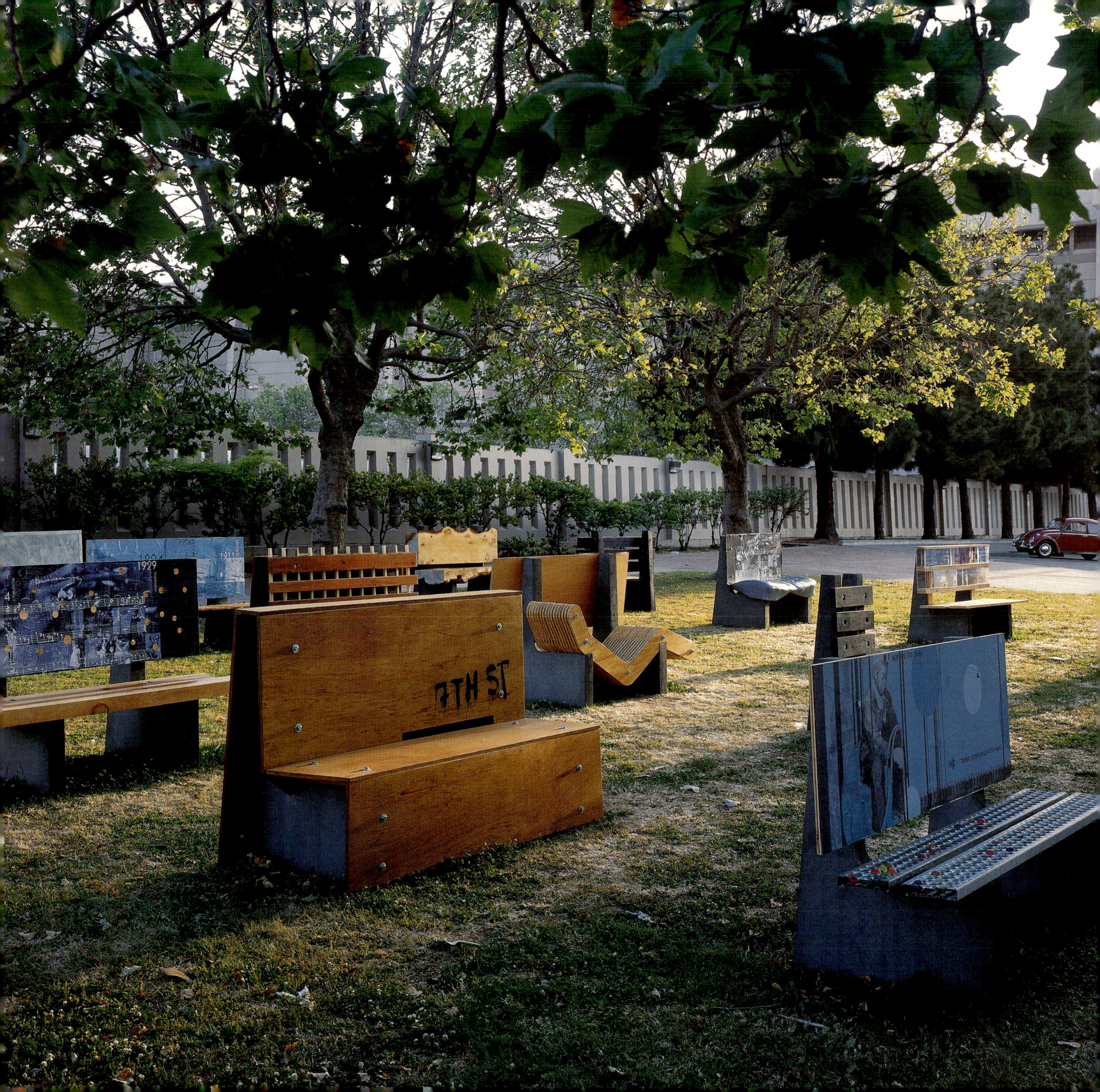
1999
7TH ST

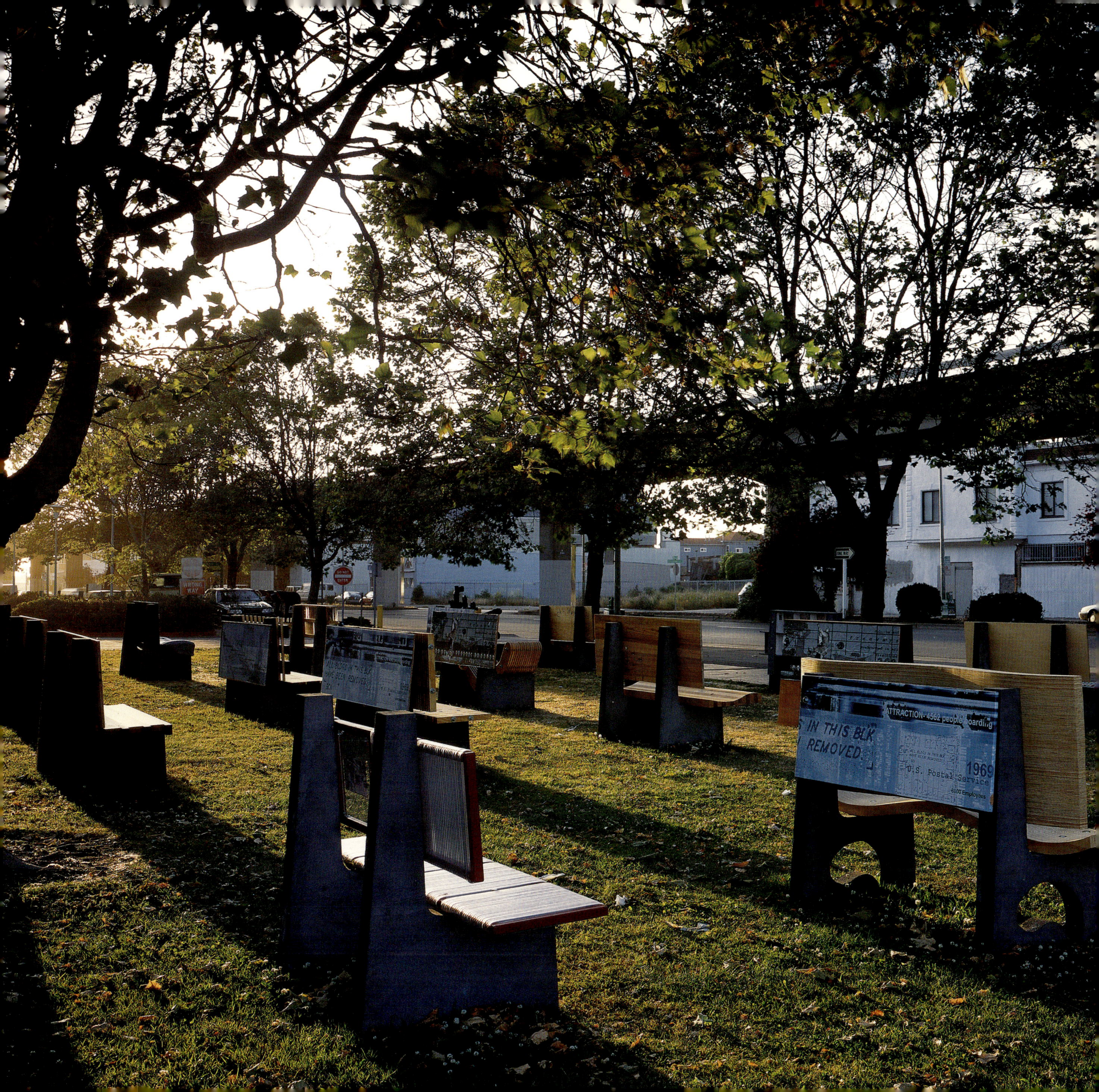
ATTRACTION- 4562 people boarding
IN THIS BLK
REMOVED.
ALL BLDGS IN THIS BLK
HAVE BEEN REMOVED
1969
U.S. Postal Service

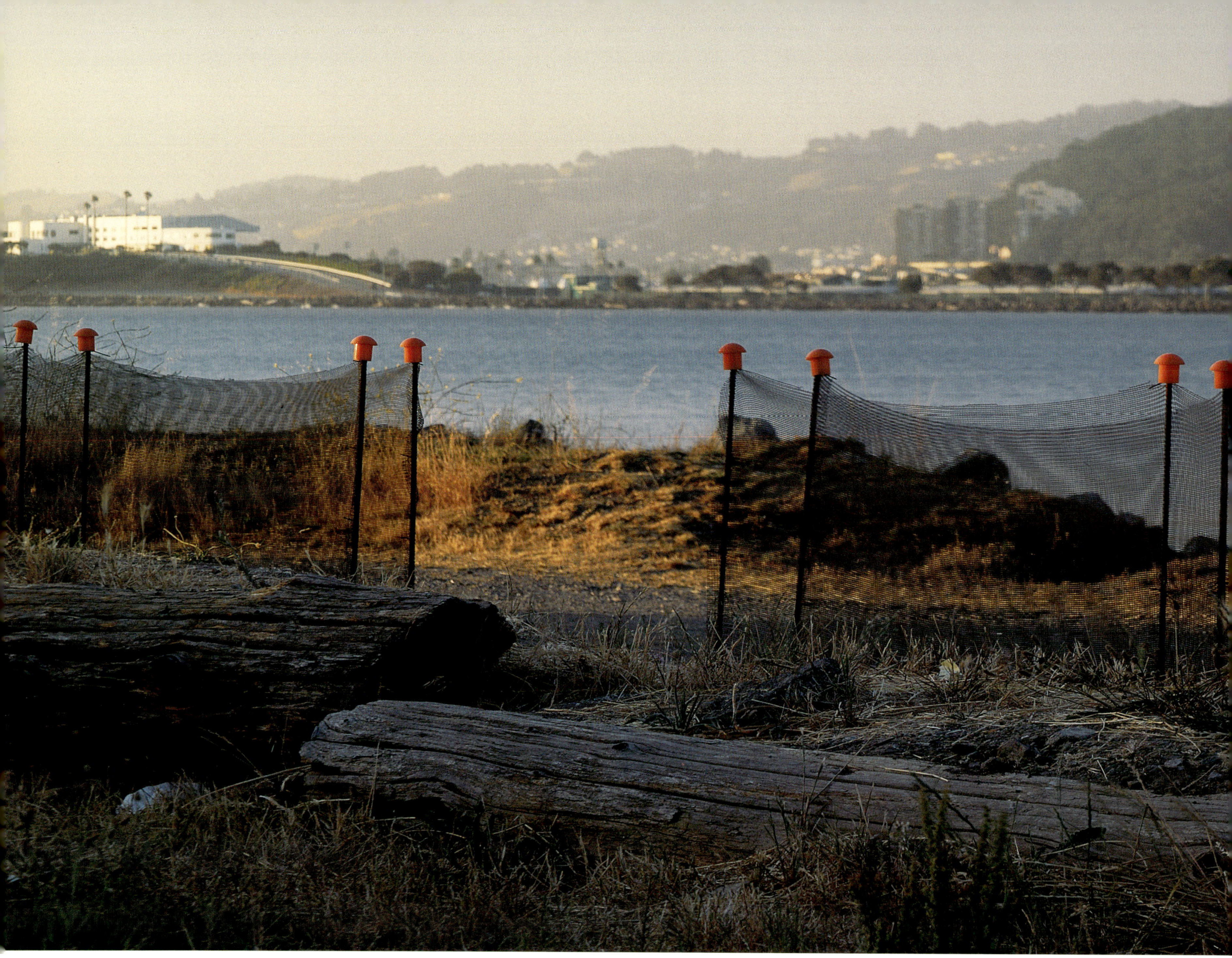

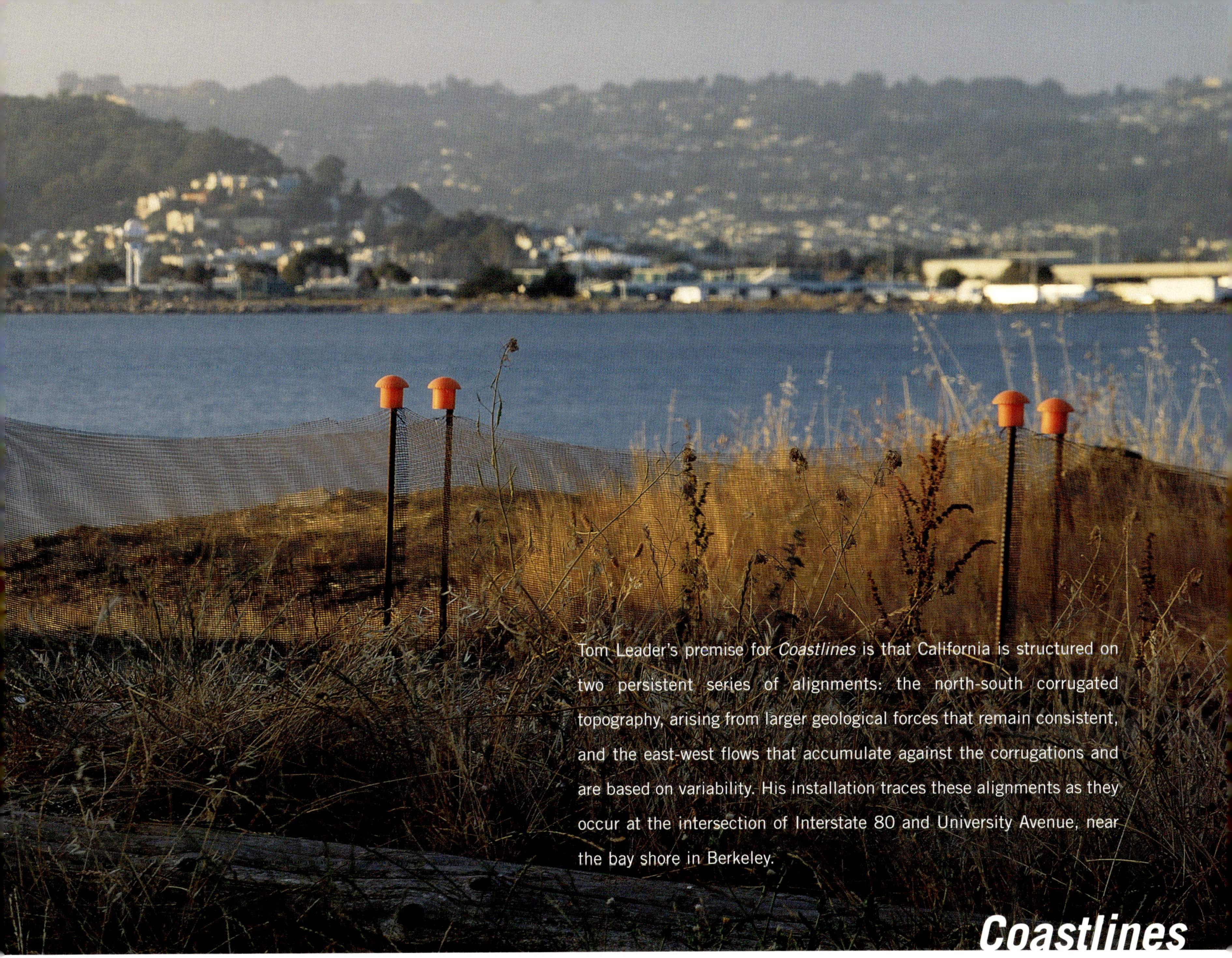

Tom Leader's premise for *Coastlines* is that California is structured on two persistent series of alignments: the north-south corrugated topography, arising from larger geological forces that remain consistent, and the east-west flows that accumulate against the corrugations and are based on variability. His installation traces these alignments as they occur at the intersection of Interstate 80 and University Avenue, near the bay shore in Berkeley.

Coastlines

Tom Leader Studio in collaboration with **Anuradha Mathur** and **Dilip da Cunha**

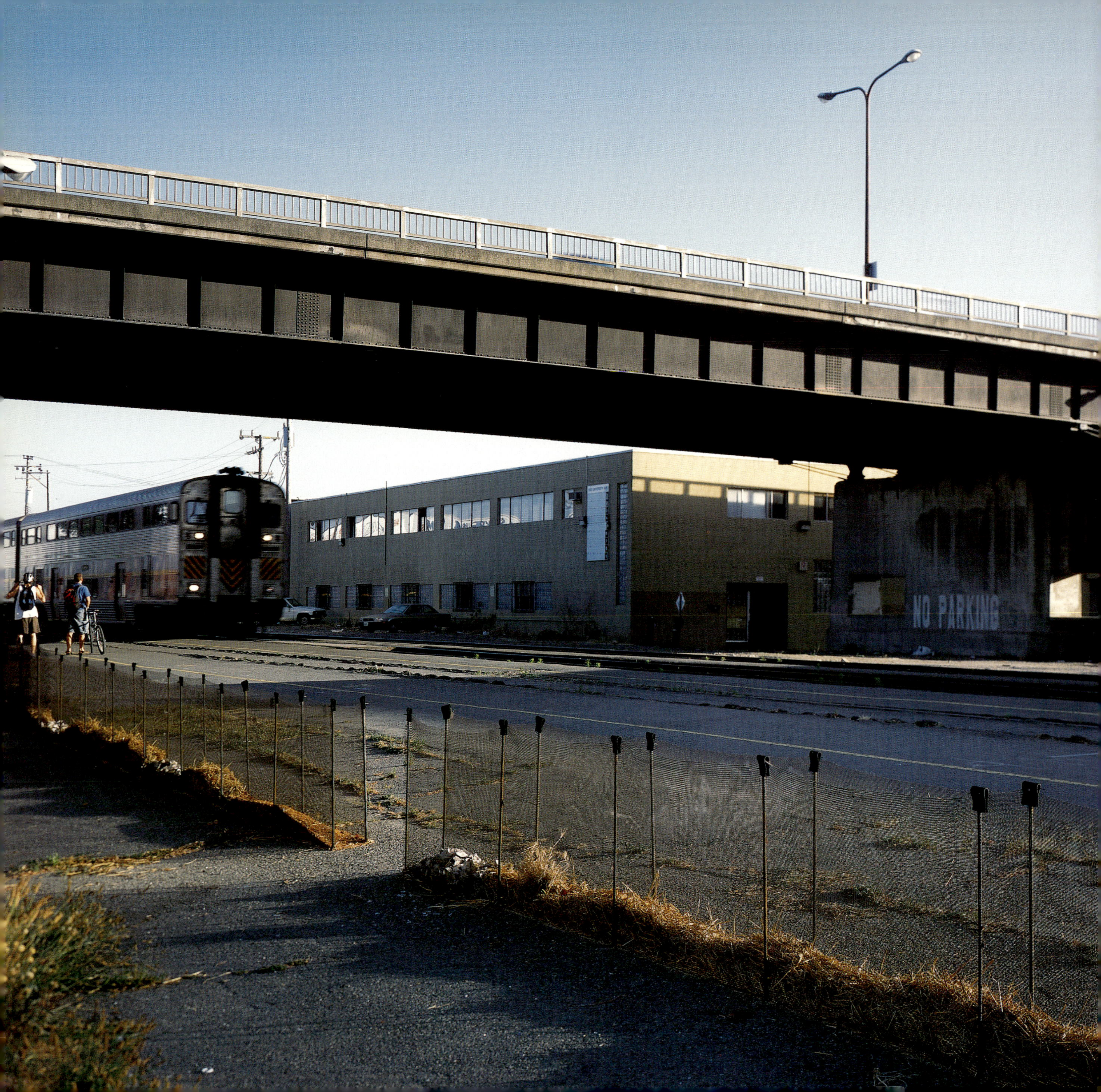
NO PARKING

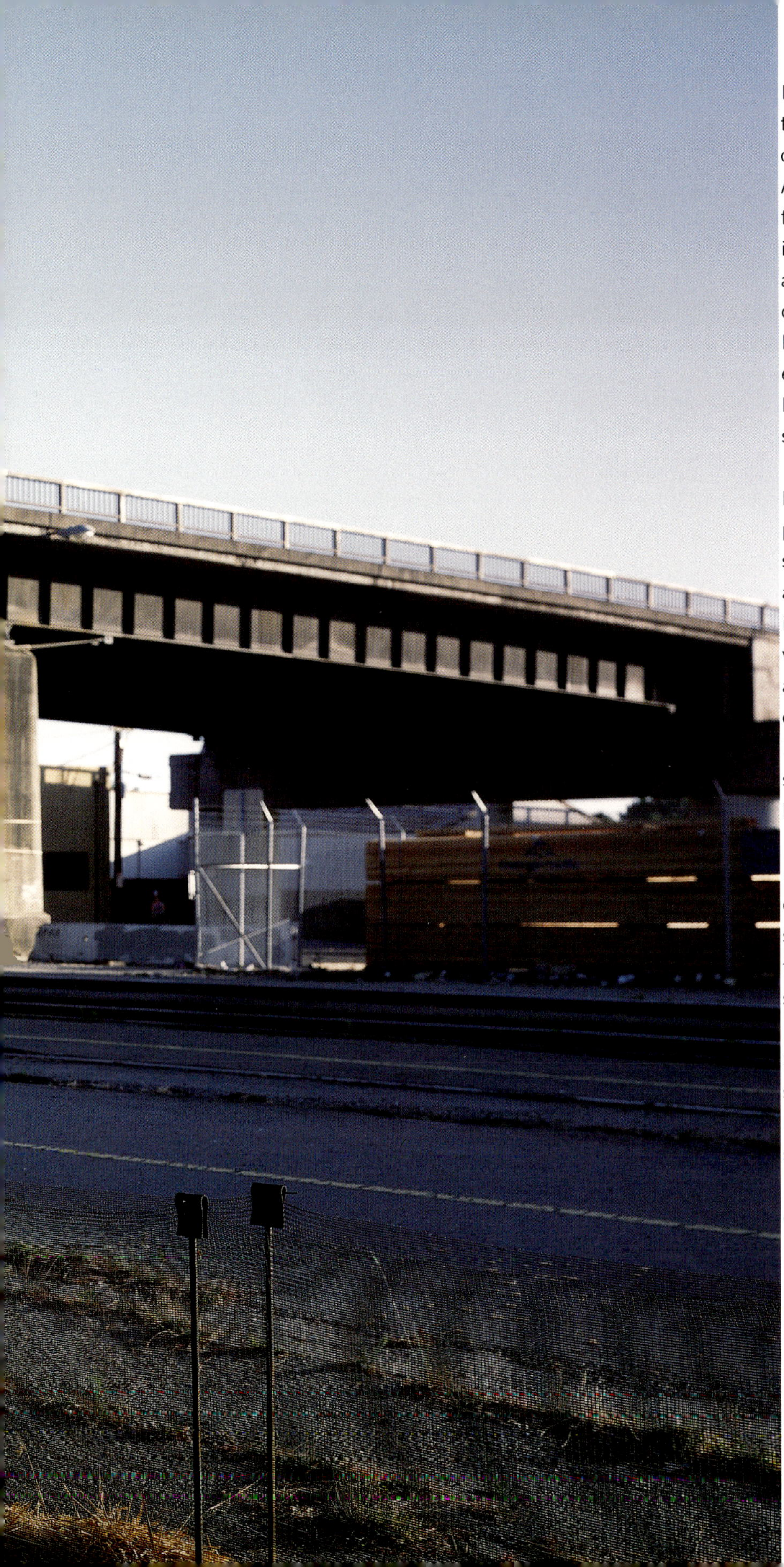

Individually potent components of the concentrated north-south system include the active Hayward earthquake fault, the bay shore, San Pablo Avenue traced over an early Spanish trail, train tracks, Interstate 80, the frontage road, and Aquatic Park, a lagoon on the east side of Interstate 80. This north-south flow of fault line, mountain, water edge, and traffic is traversed by more occasional and isolated east-west events: the Berkeley Pier, which at one point extended three and one-half miles into the bay, the pervasive fog that blows in from the ocean during the summer months, the Bay and San Rafael Bridges, which connect the East Bay to land farther west and north, and the Caldecott Tunnel, which burrows east through the mountains. Leader and his collaborators, Anuradha Mathur and Dilip da Cunha, view these striated surfaces, some natural and some artificial, as significant experiences of the "edge of the country."

For *Coastlines*, the team created a kind of urban nature trail that makes each person who follows it a part of the east-west flow pattern, thereby heightening a sense of the topography in a visceral and immediate way. To map the north-south alignments through the one-mile-long installation, Leader has created an intermittent, three-dimensional screen from two vertical lines of ordinary black vinyl screening attached to three-foot-high poles and placed about nine inches apart. Each of the four screen lines is filled with various materials that relate to or are generated by the installation's terrain: oyster shells that refer to a historic Native American shell mound, sawdust and ground wood from the lumberyard, shredded paper, plastic placards, concrete and asphalt chunks, newspaper bundles, plastic bottles, shredded tires, eco-compost, and seeds.

Coastlines can be experienced through many encounters at different times or in one visit. People who live nearby or who frequent the area may come across sections of the screen line at various points. The first line parallels the railroad tracks, where the derelict landscape is in sharp contrast to the upscale walks and shops of the popular Fourth Street neighborhood just a few blocks away. Here day laborers typically gather for pickup work at the intersection of Hearst and Third Streets. Nearby, at the foot of University Avenue, a dark and seemingly abandoned space under the freeway serves as the unlikely bus and Amtrak stop. The second north-south screen line parallels Bolivar Drive and marks the original bay shoreline, now the edge of Aquatic Park. The installation along this typically quiet lagoon coincides with the construction of a new, larger pedestrian bridge leading over Interstate 80.

The investigation moves west, crossing the freeway at University Avenue, to the third north-south screen line, which follows the curve of West Frontage Road at the edge of the Eastshore Regional Park. The contrast between the marked isolation of this area and the experience of walking over Interstate 80 generates immediate and varied reactions on the part of visitors: the thunder and speed of cars rushing under the elevated pedestrian bridge, the danger of traversing a freeway off-ramp, the proximity of nature and infrastructure, the pounding noise of construction interspersed with birdsongs from the protected shoreline sanctuary all unfold in a rapid succession that is both confusing and exhilarating.

The last of the *Coastlines* screen lines is one-third of a mile west at the end of University Avenue, passing in front of a Radisson Hotel along the road to Cesar Chavez Park. The experience of the topography culminates in a view back toward the tremendous scarp of the Hayward fault looming in the hills to the east.

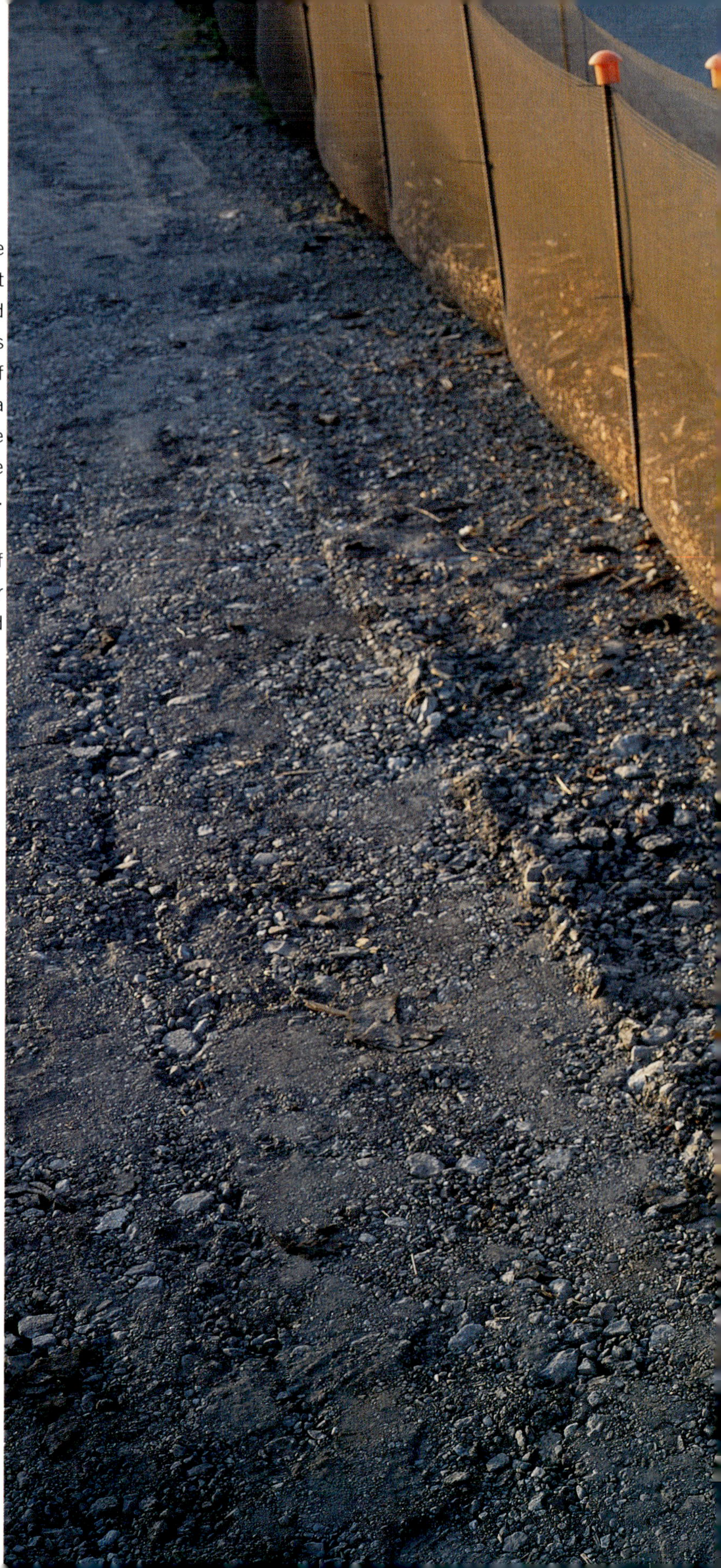

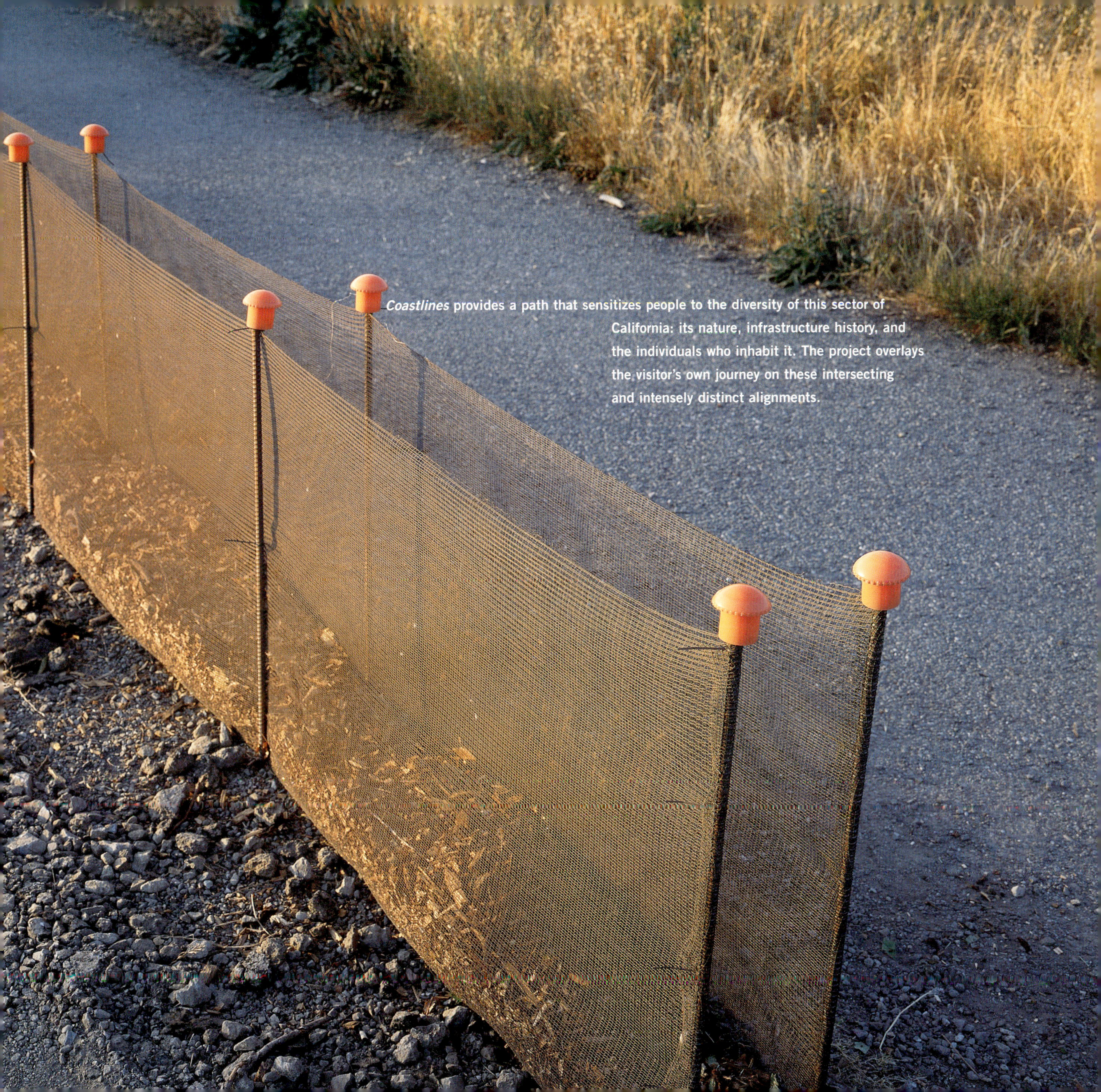

Coastlines provides a path that sensitizes people to the diversity of this sector of California: its nature, infrastructure history, and the individuals who inhabit it. The project overlays the visitor's own journey on these intersecting and intensely distinct alignments.

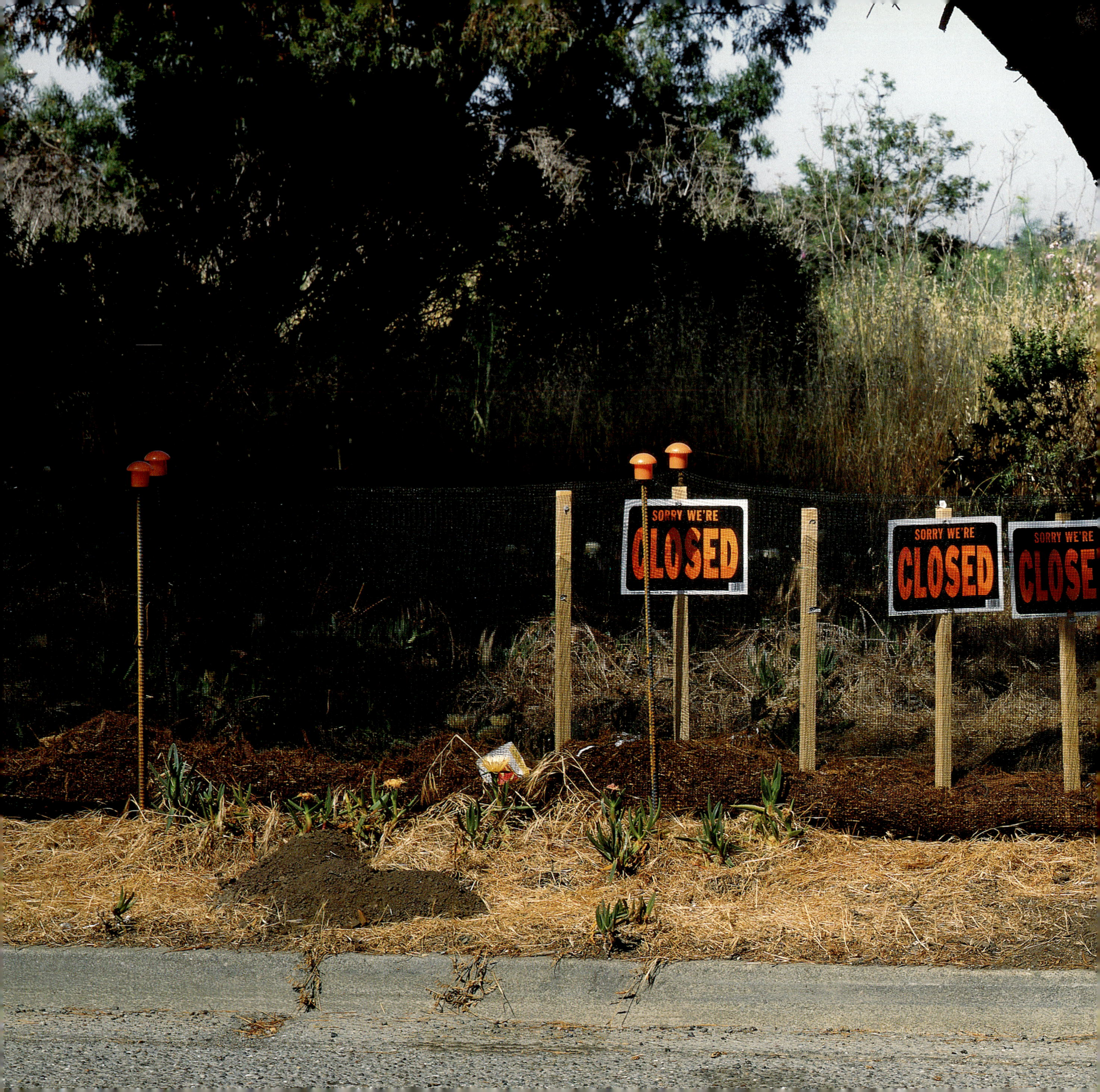
SORRY WE'RE
CLOSED
SORRY WE'RE
CLOSED
SORRY WE'RE
CLOSE

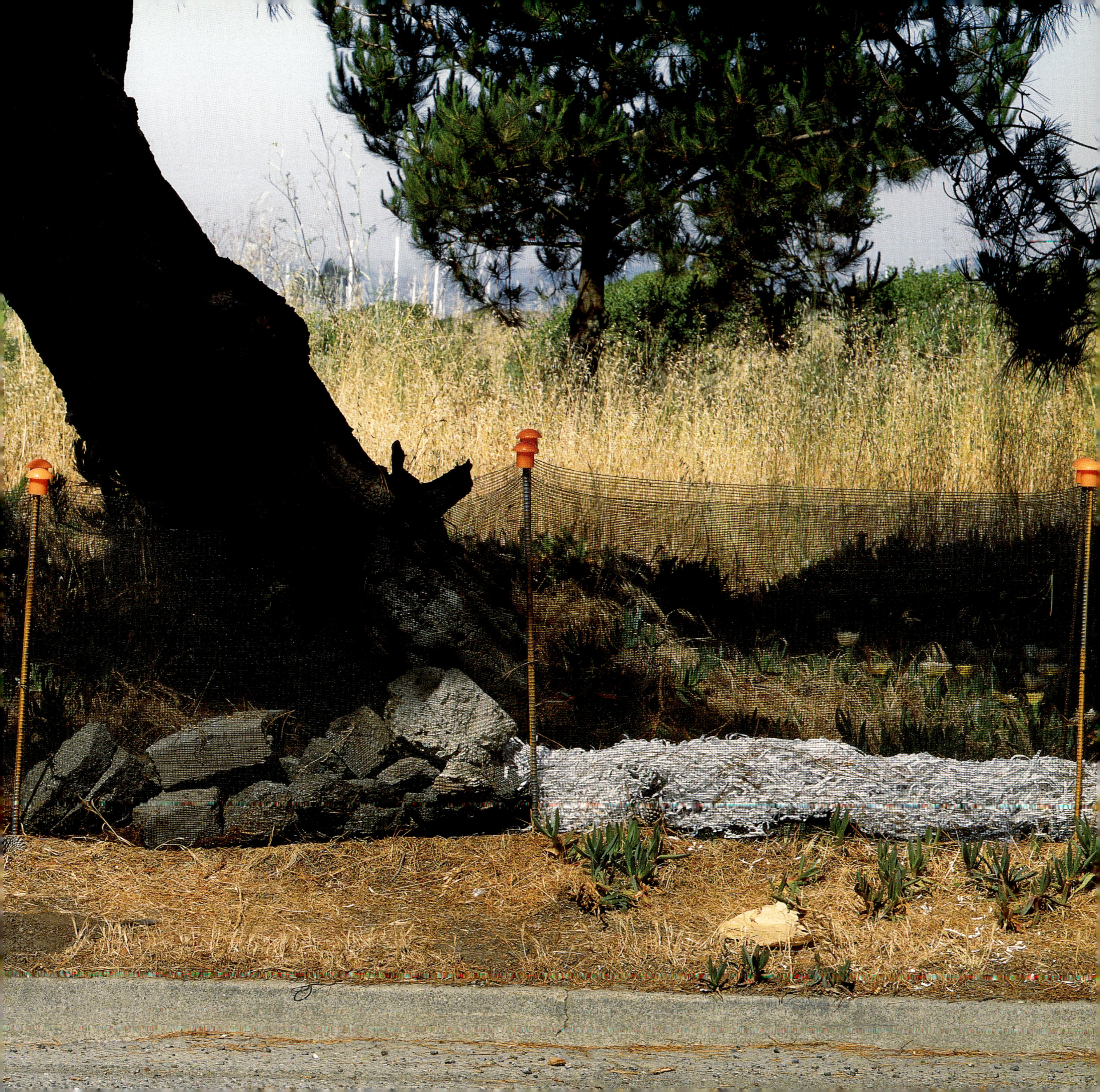

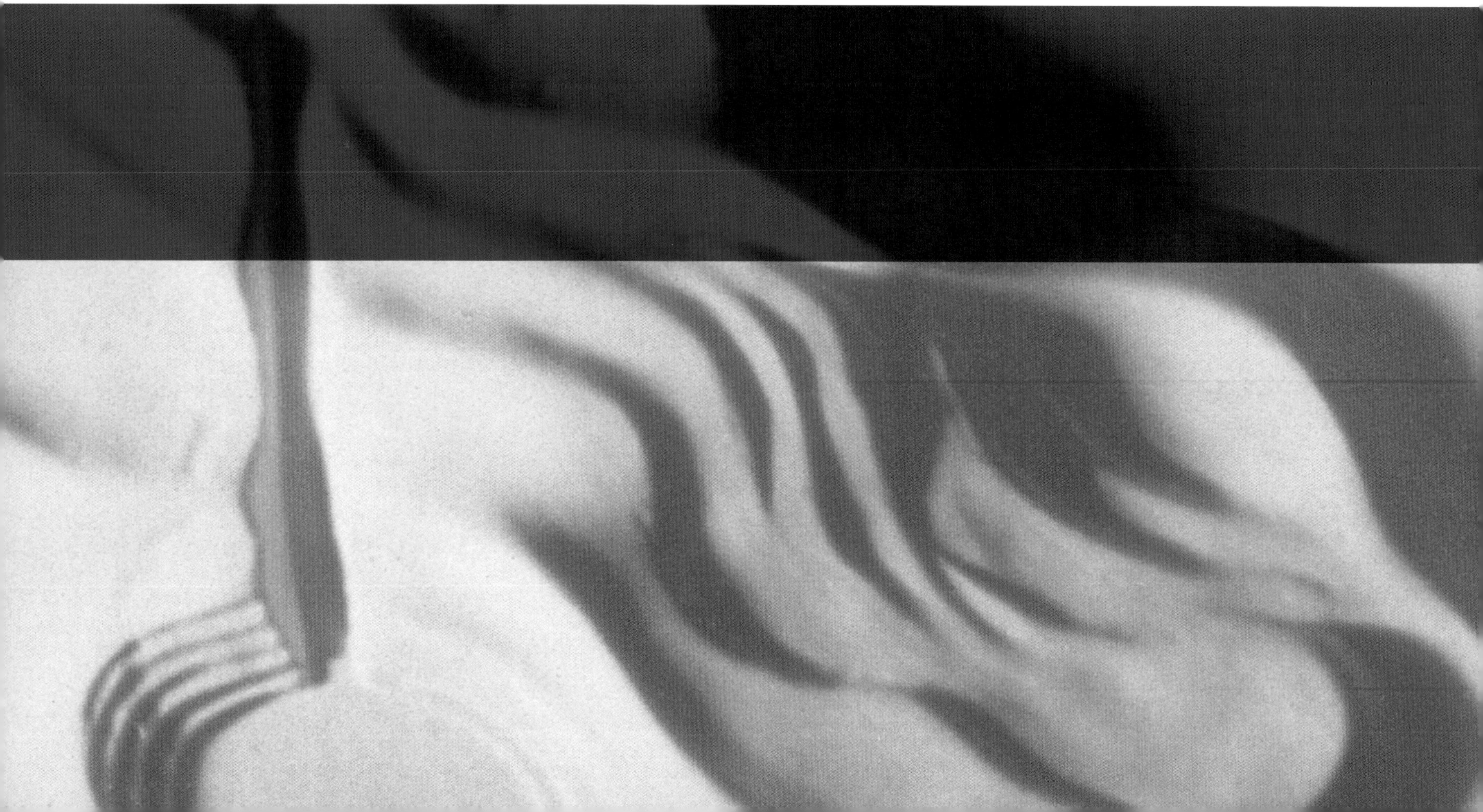

Text by **Leah Levy**

Kathryn Gustafson **Hargreaves Associates** **Walter Hood** **Tom Leader**

PREVIOUS WORK

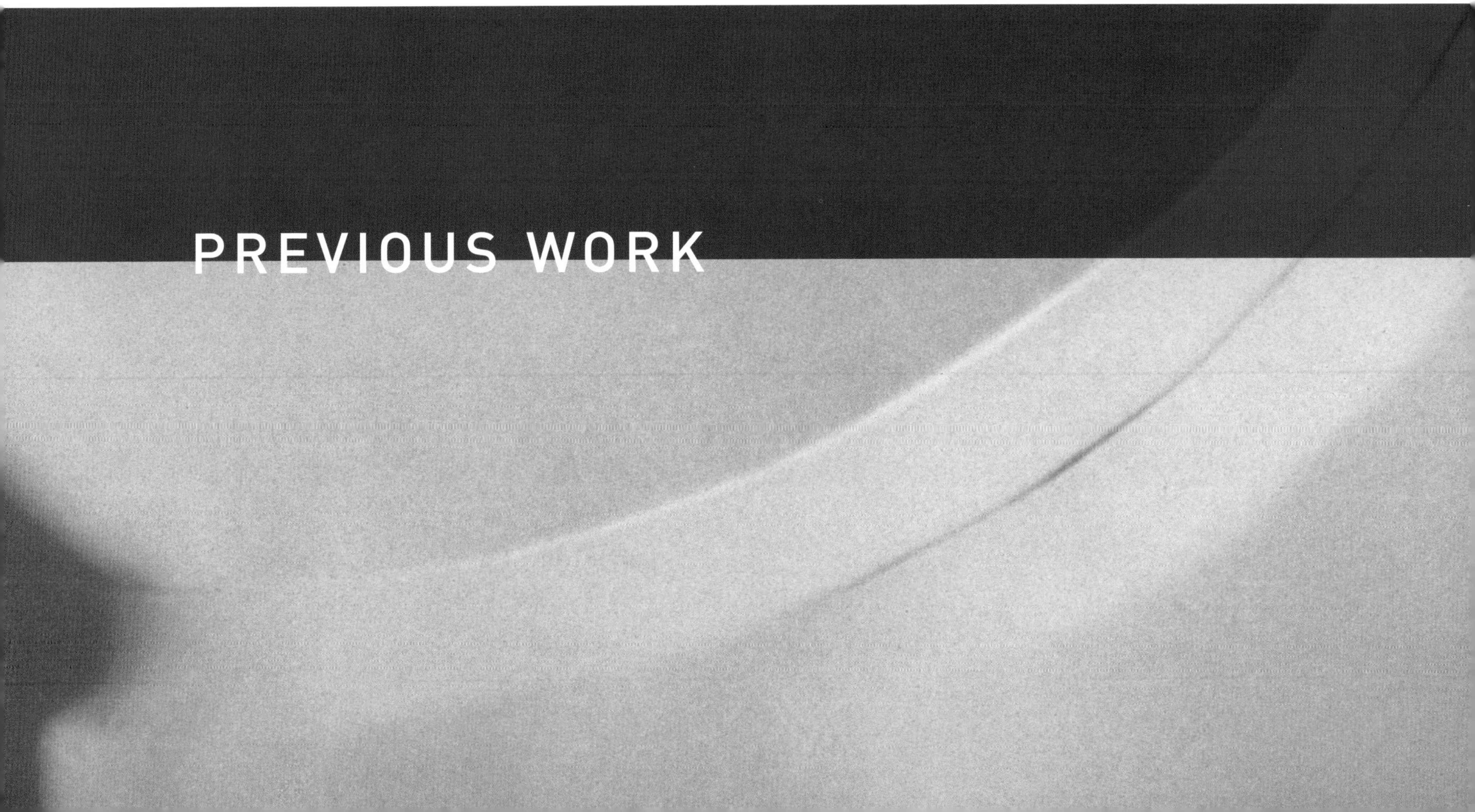

KATHRYN GUSTAFSON

Often conceived on an epic scale, Kathryn Gustafson's work has claimed a unique place in contemporary landscape design. Prior to earning a degree in landscape design, Gustafson studied textile design, and this early interest is reflected in the use of drape, curve, and dramatic dimension in her landscapes. It was in France, where she lived and worked for more than twenty years, designing primarily corporate and civic spaces, that her work first won recognition for its sensuous forms, intricate plantings, and sculptural use of natural materials.

Gustafson finds inspiration for her designs in the depths of her own emotions and experiences and seeks to make them accessible and meaningful to people. Although her design process is deeply personal and introspective, the work itself is often of monumental scale and created at extremely challenging and problematic sites.

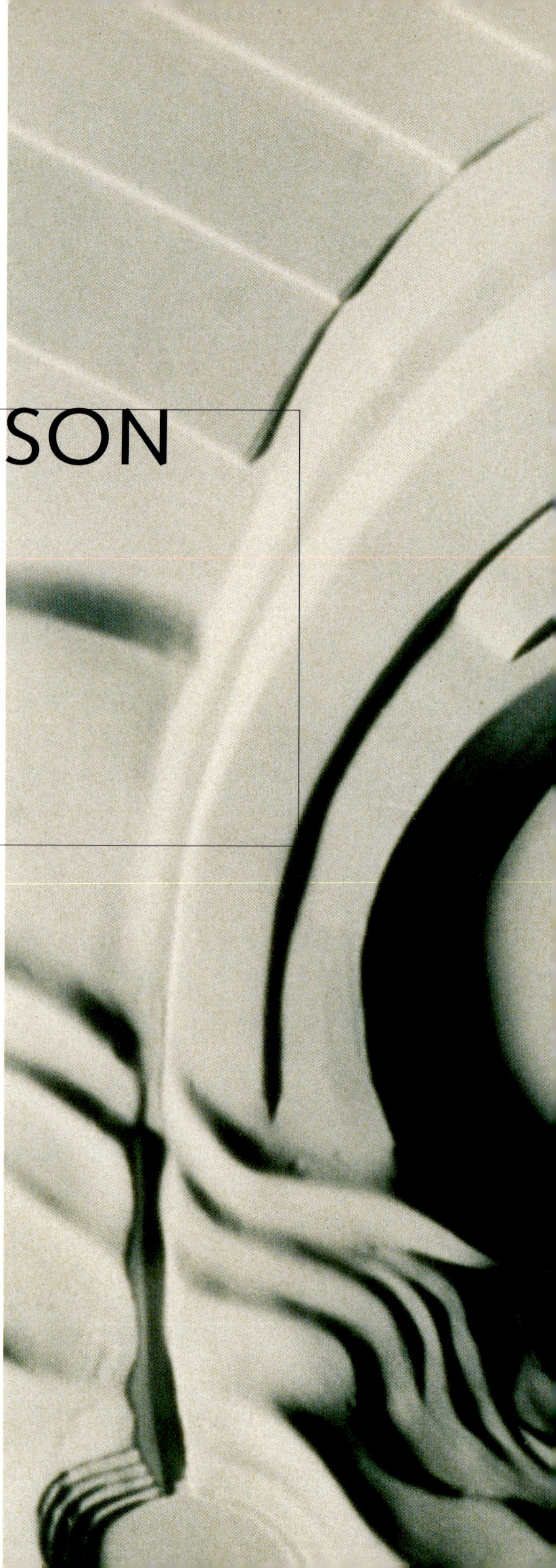

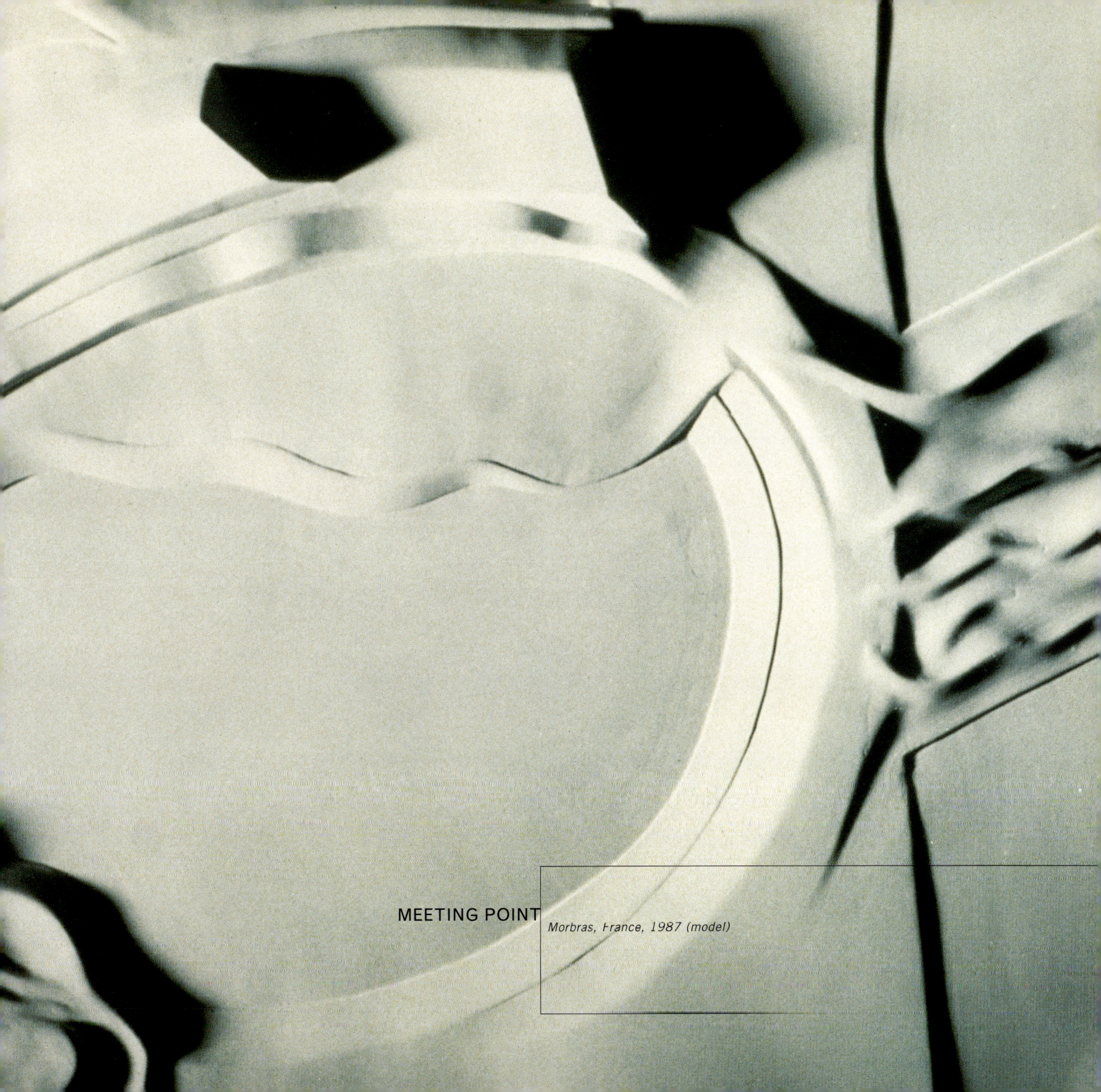

MEETING POINT

Morbras, France, 1987 (model)

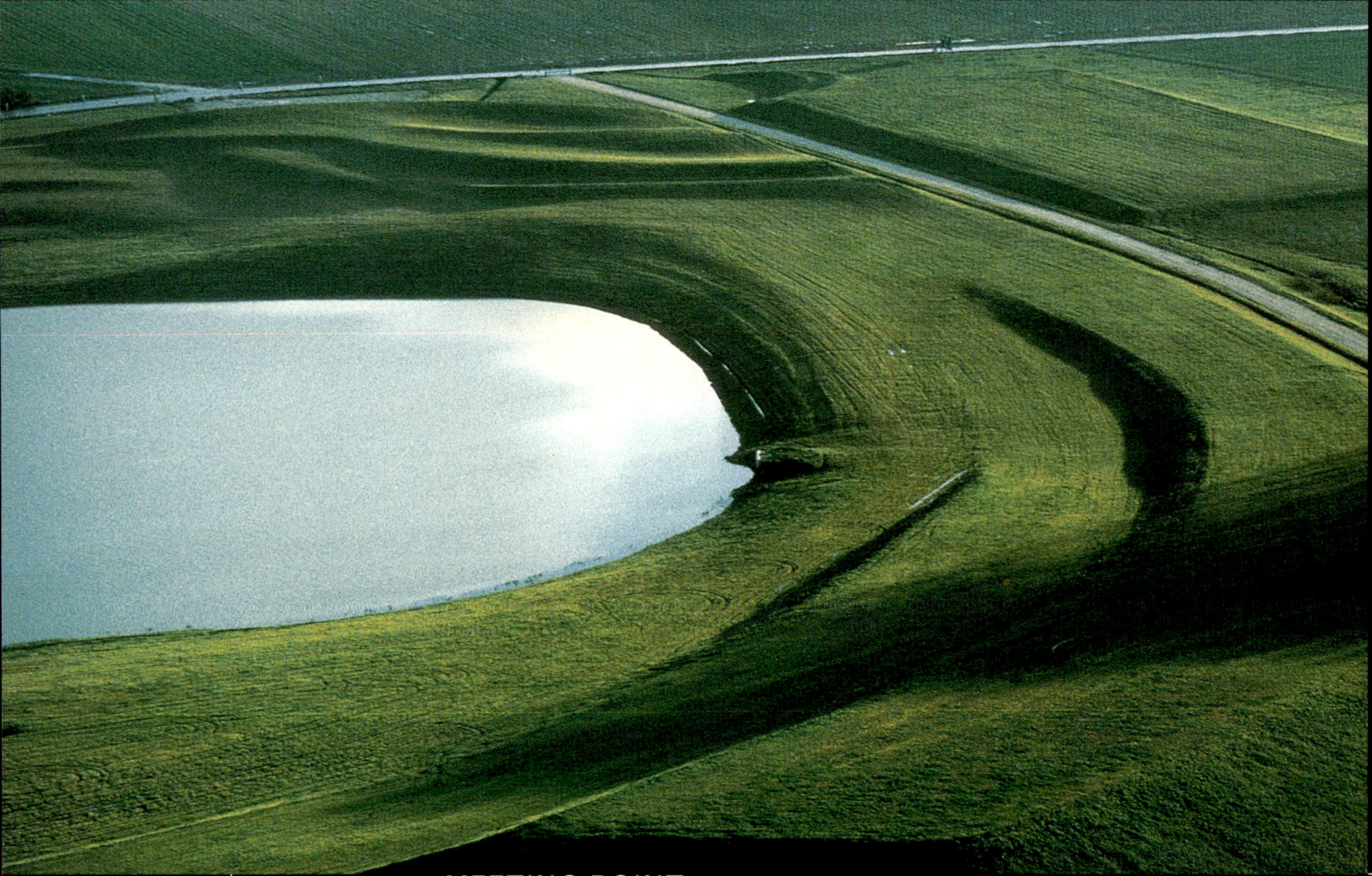

MEETING POINT

Morbras, France, 1987

At Morbras, south of Paris, Gustafson used four hundred thousand cubic yards of excavated earth displaced from the creation of a reservoir to sculpt a park that undulates around the newly created body of water.

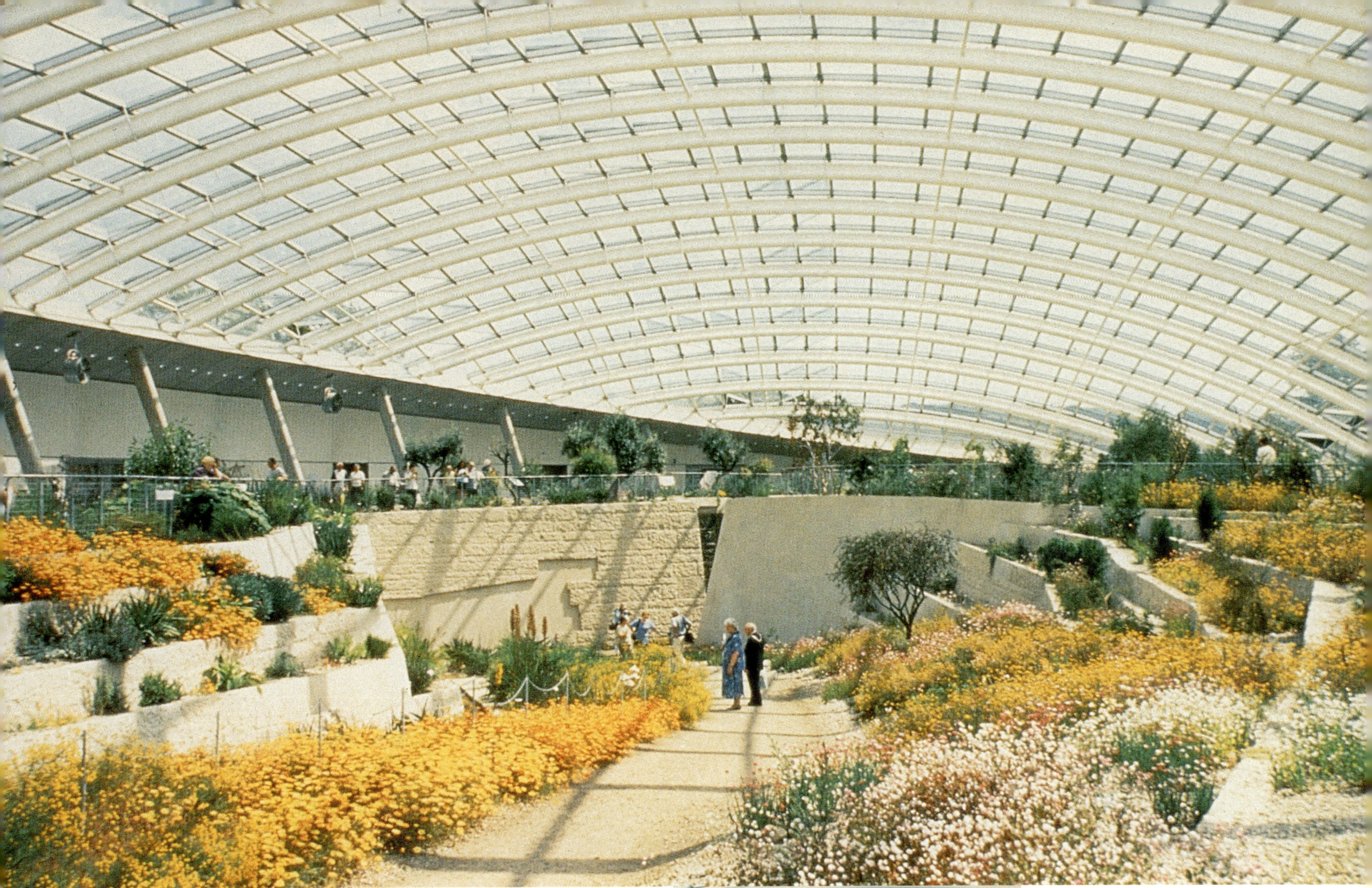

GREAT GLASS HOUSE

The National Botanic Garden of Wales

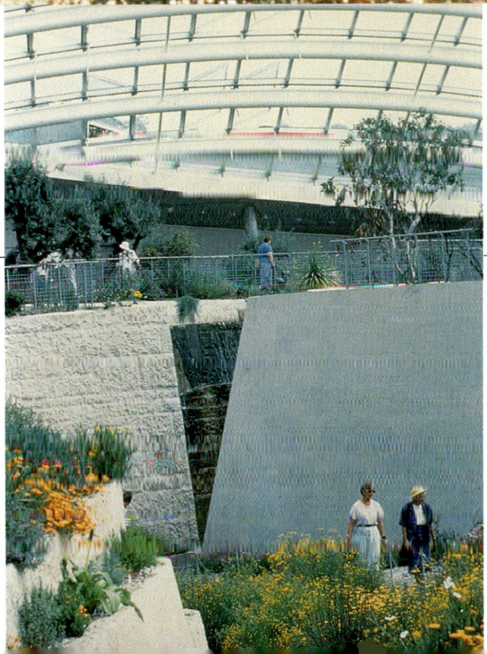

Carmarthenshire, Wales, 2000

Gustafson designed a sculptural landscape in the spectacular Glass House of the National Botanic Garden of Wales, using an earthen ravine six feet deep to delineate the spaces and scale of the indoor landscape.

Terrasson, France, 1995

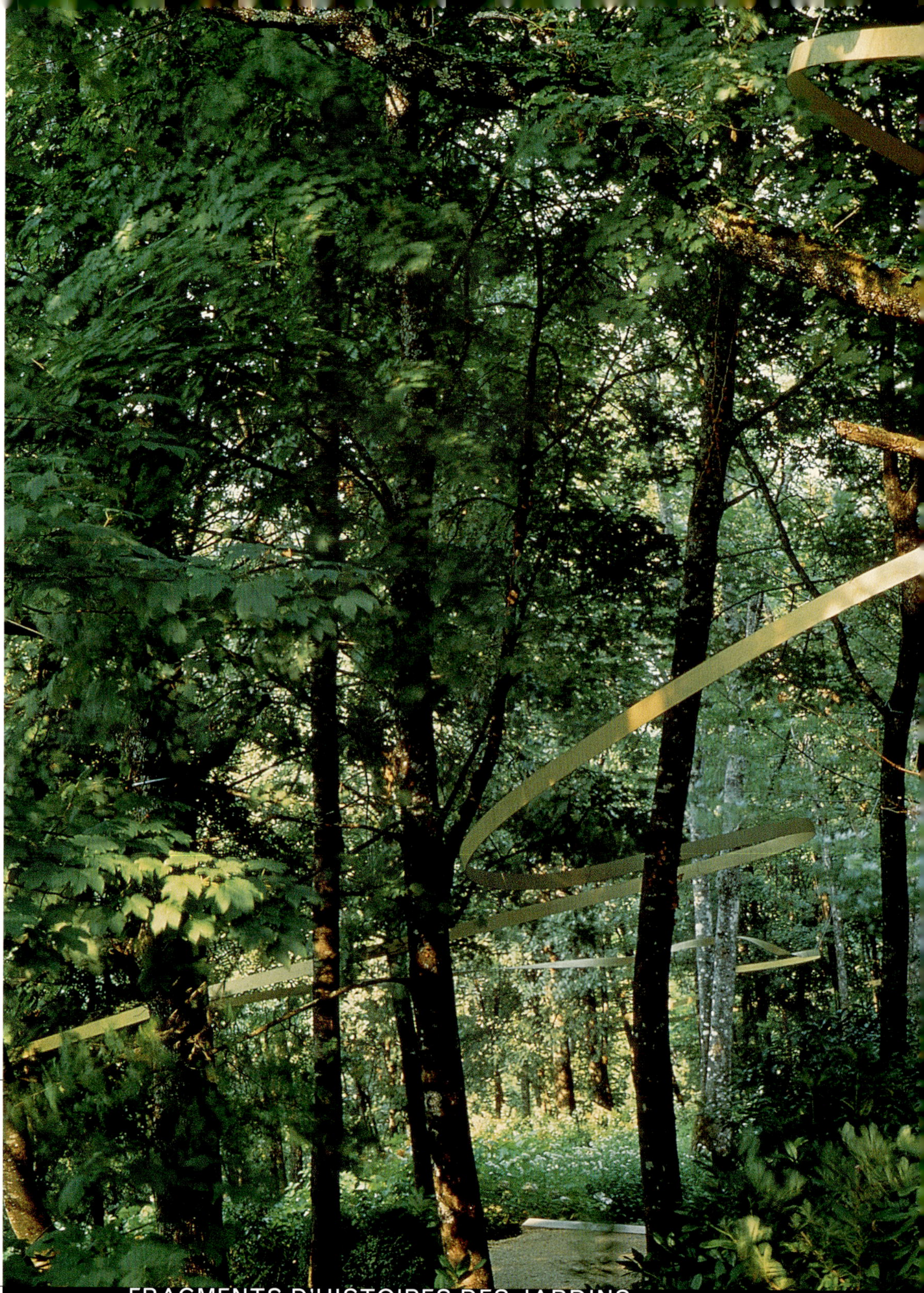

FRAGMENTS D'HISTOIRES DES JARDINS

(Fragments of Garden History)

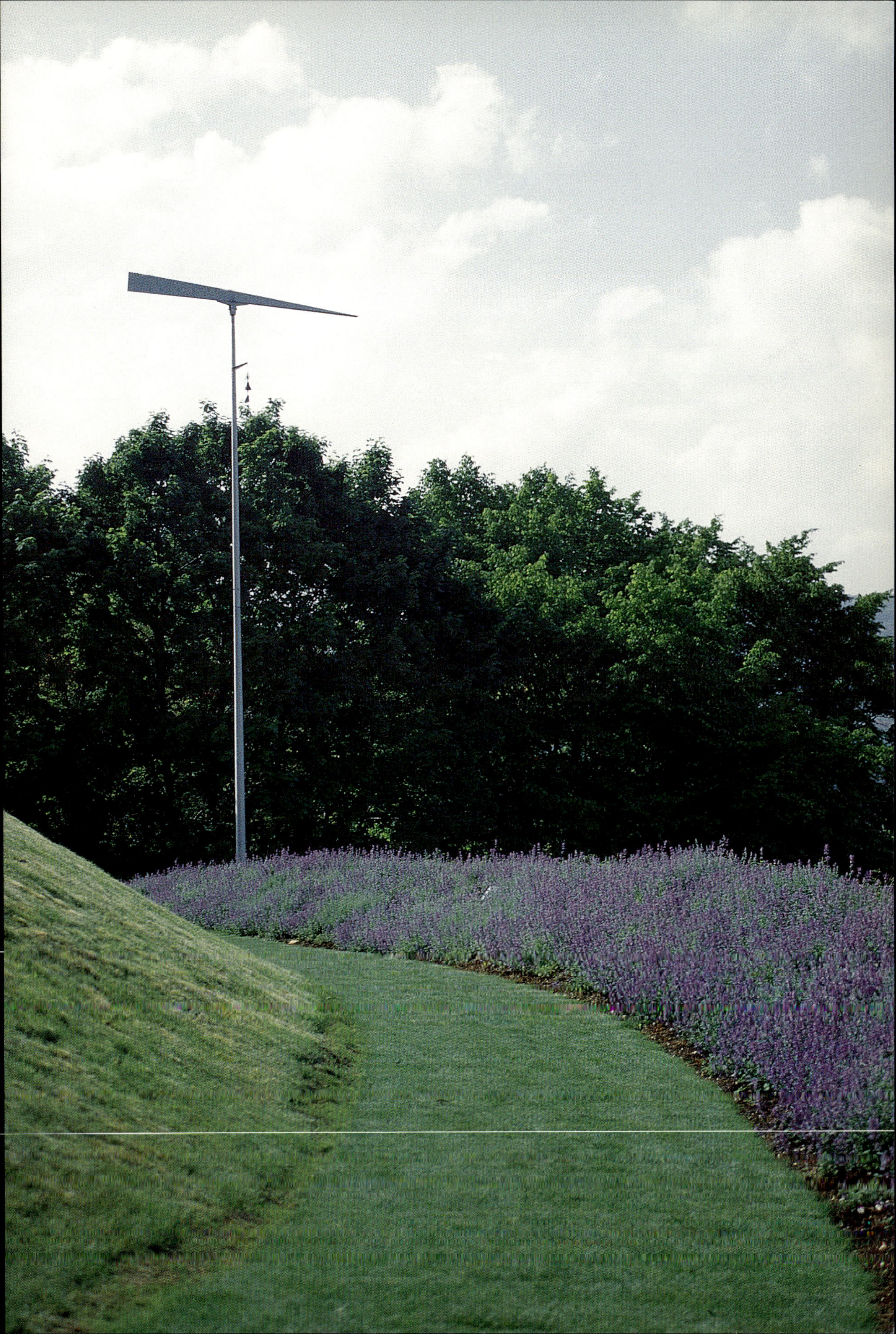

Gustafson's design for a park overlooking the historic village of Terrasson comprises a series of spaces and walks, with areas named Axis of the Wind, the Element Garden, History Boxed, and Ephemeral Tracings.

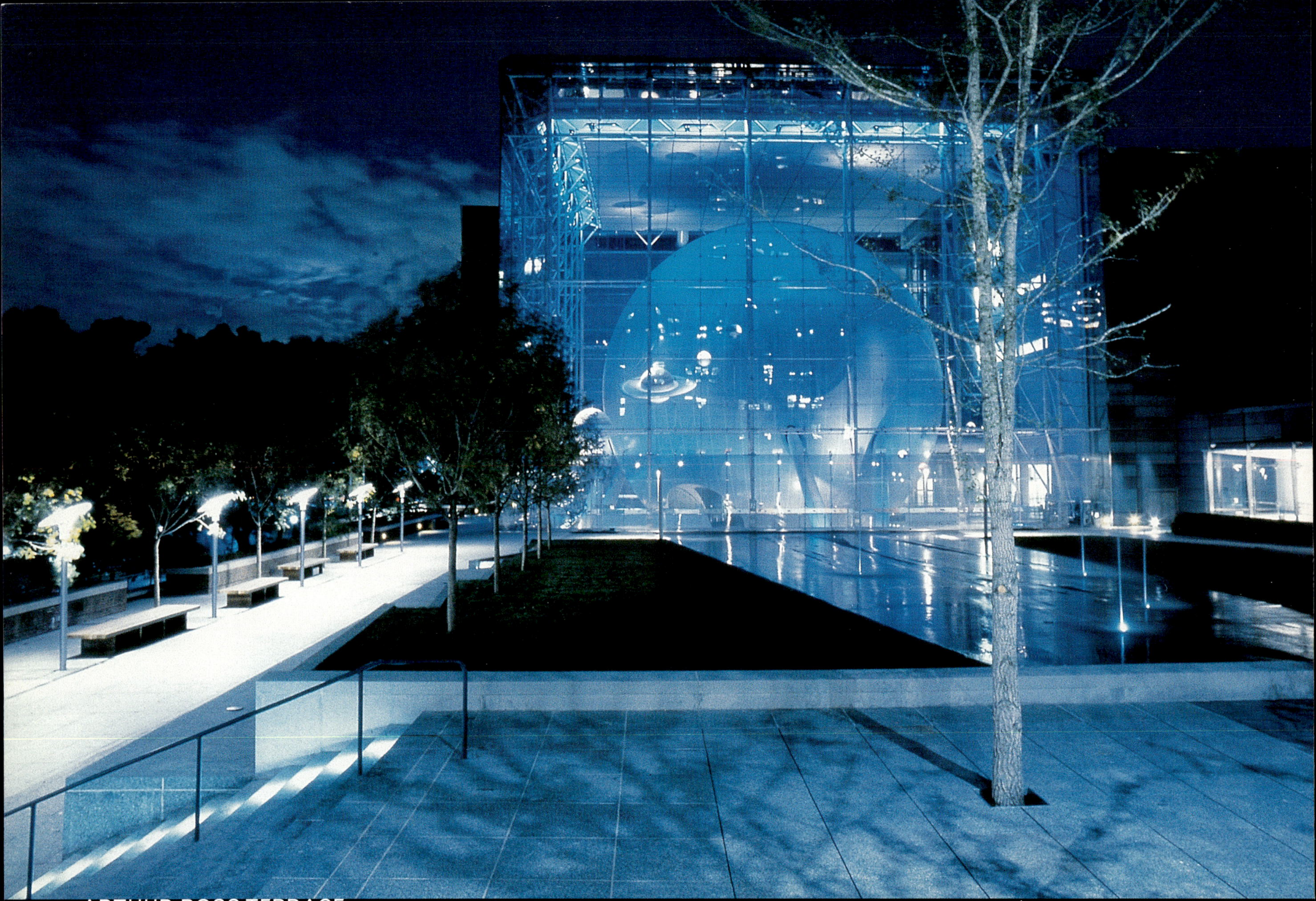

ARTHUR ROSS TERRACE

Rose Center for Earth and Space, American Museum of Natural History

New York, New York, 2000

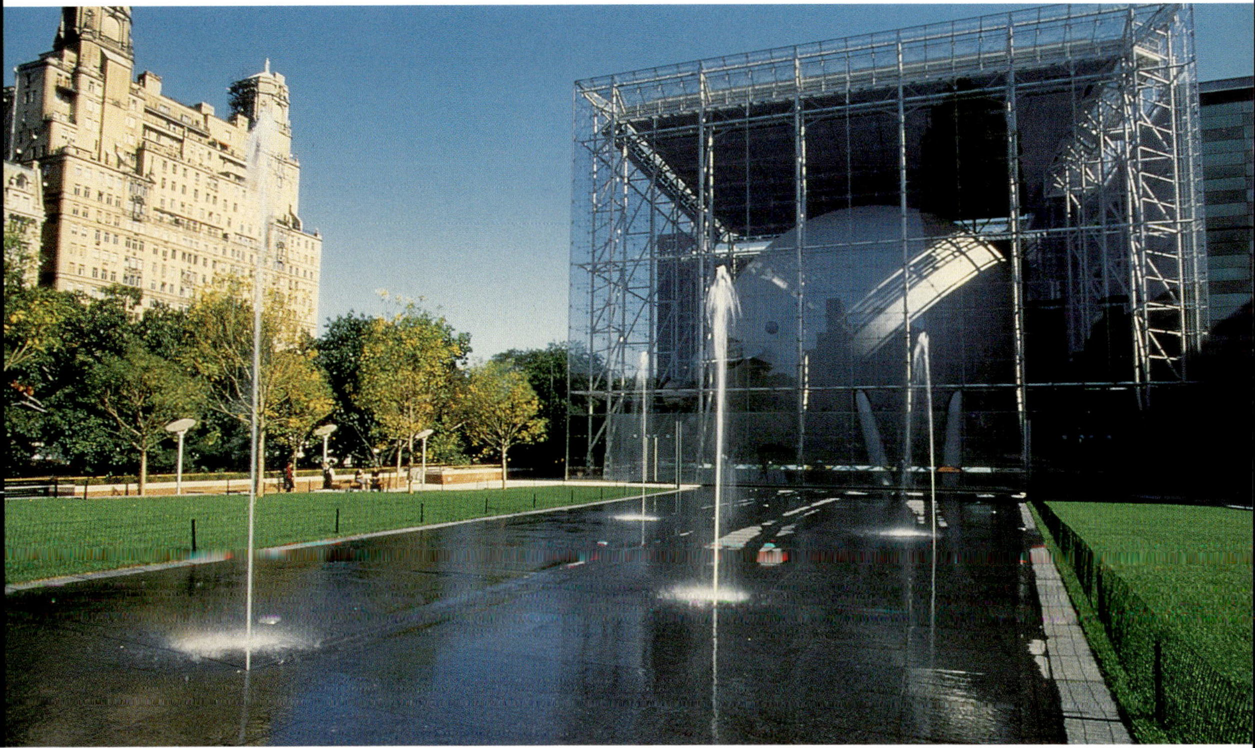

For an outdoor plaza bridging the new Rose Center for Earth and Space with the existing structure of the American Museum of Natural History, Gustafson designed a dramatic landscape suggesting moon shadows cast onto the plaza from within the Hayden Planetarium.

HARGREAVES ASSOCIATES

our work deals
with land
which has been made
and re-made

For two decades Mary Margaret Jones and George Hargreaves of Hargreaves Associates have followed the premise that landscape design can reveal the essential nature of a site. On hostile natural areas or in undeveloped spaces, often along urban edges or bodies of water, their work builds, on a grand scale, on their belief that "made" landscapes are never really natural. "With increasing frequency, our work deals with land which has been made and re-made," states Jones. The revelatory process employed in Hargreaves Associates' local and international projects involves reconnecting human experience of the land through multilayered landscapes, where human intervention or neglect indicates the extent to which people value their land.

The firm has tackled projects that reclaim derelict landscapes by means of a kind of archaeology, unearthing both the physical and cultural attributes of abandoned sites and remaking them for public use. "The truths that are uncovered in the analysis of environmental phenomenon should be fodder—the subject—of design," says Hargreaves.

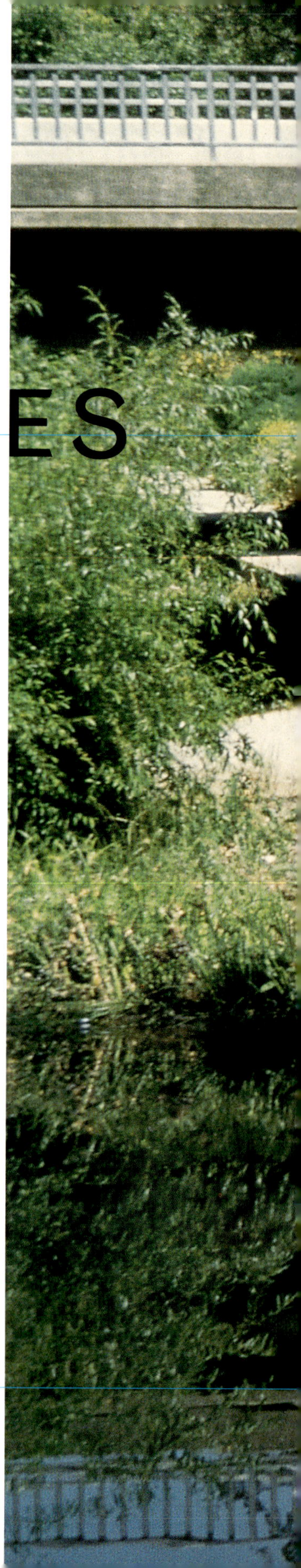

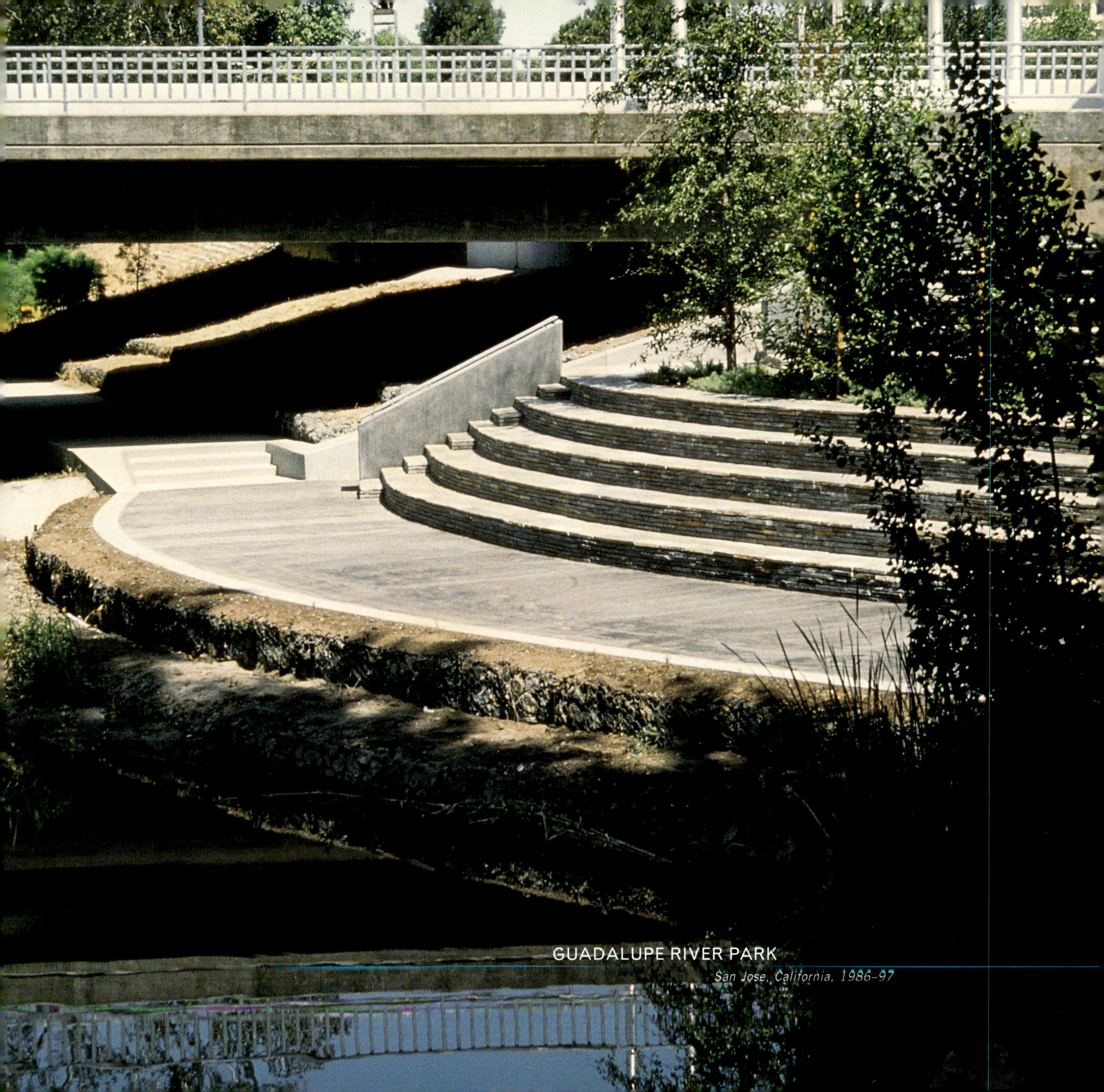

GUADALUPE RIVER PARK

San Jose, California, 1986–97

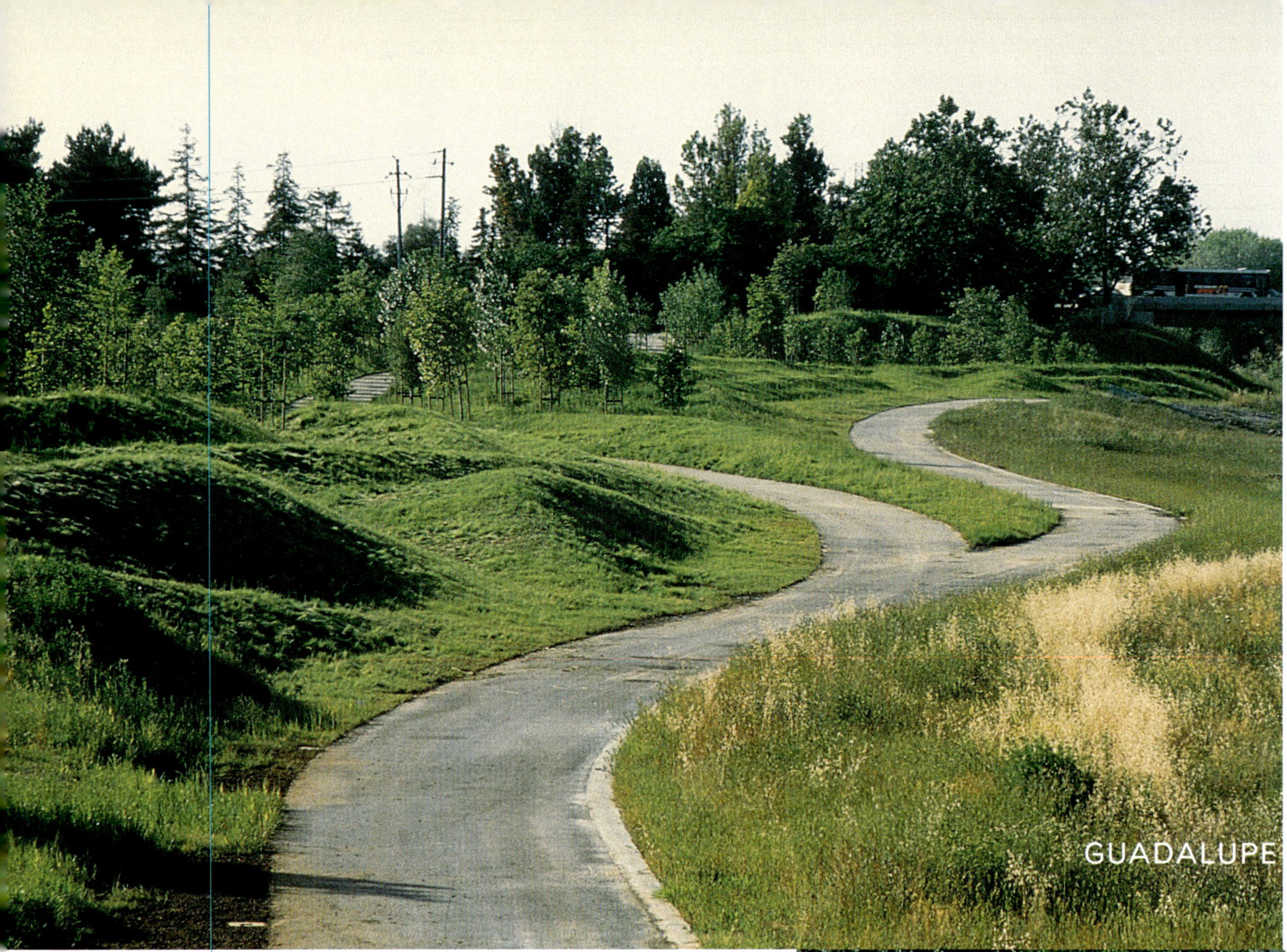

GUADALUPE RIVER PARK

San Jose, California, 1986–97

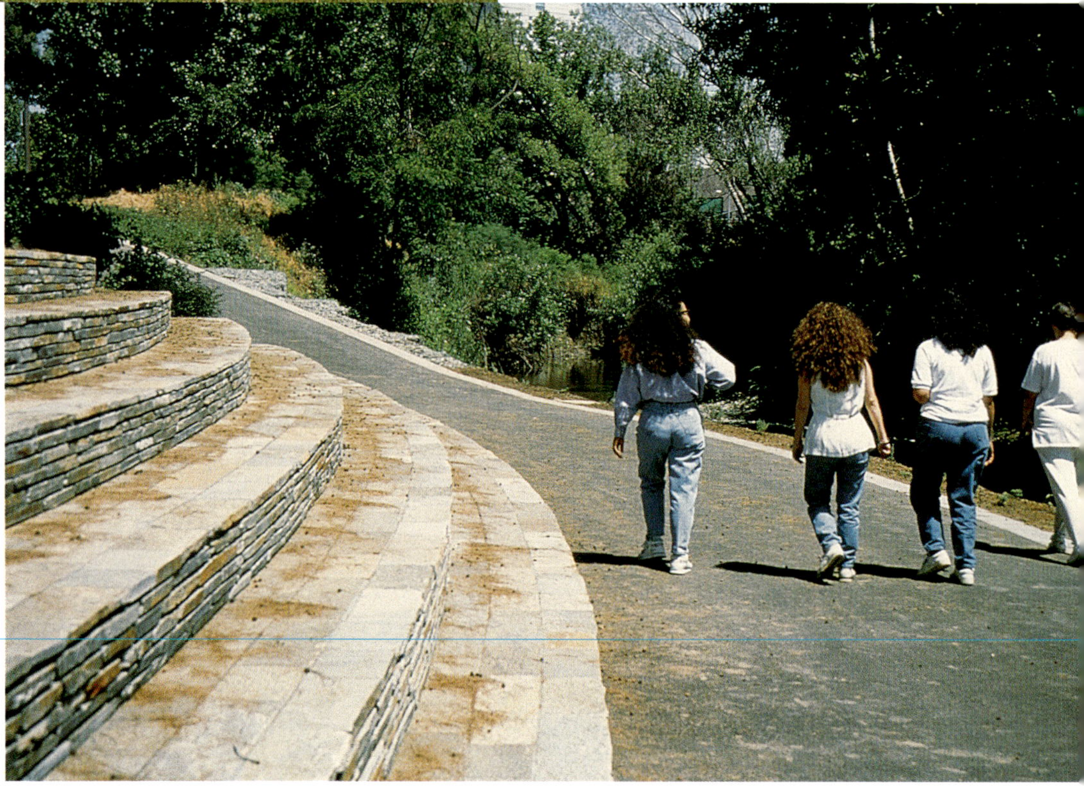

Hargreaves Associates' creation of the three-mile linear Guadalupe River Park that extends through downtown San Jose has revitalized the community by controlling the flood zone and creating a series of beautiful and usable public open spaces.

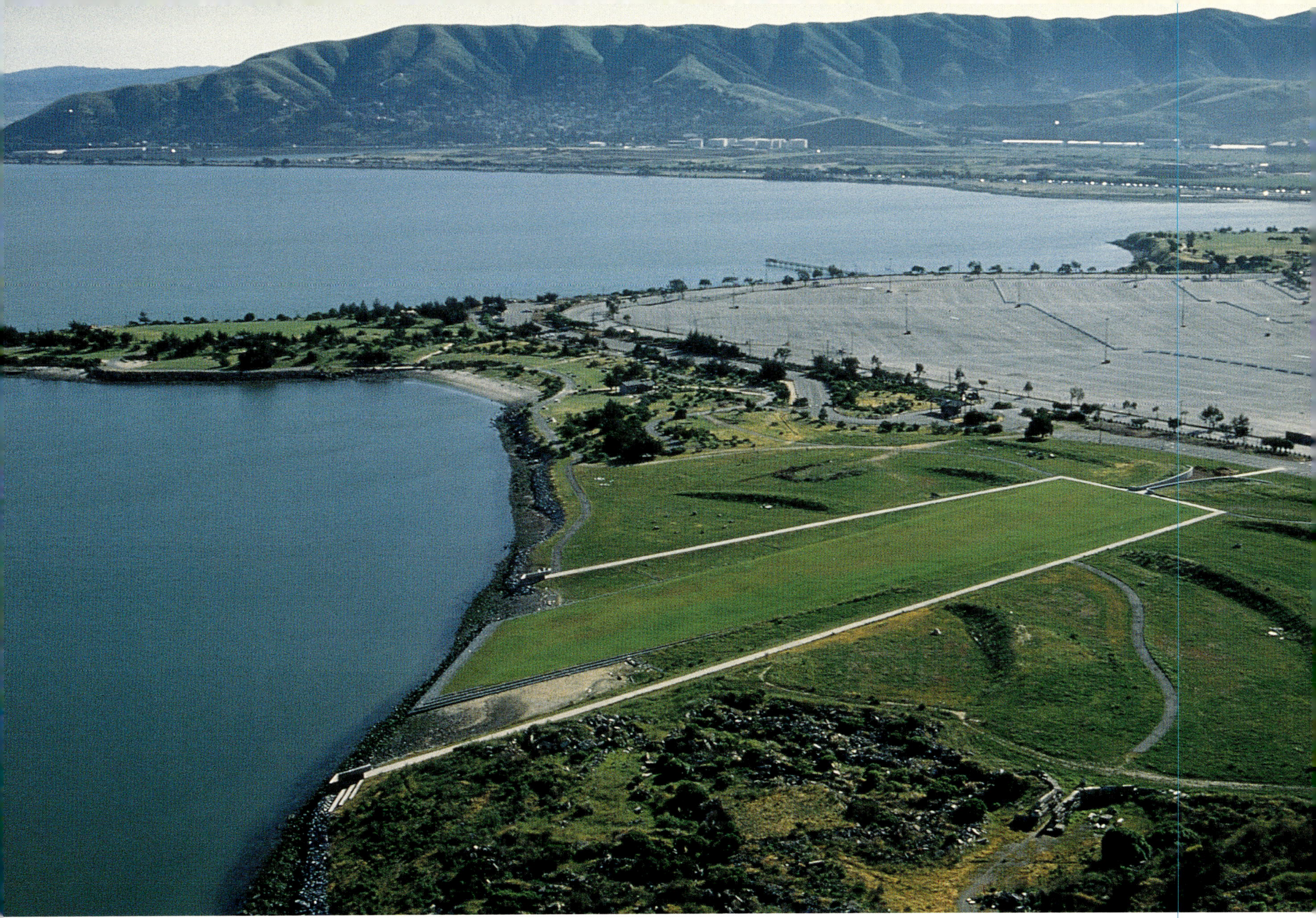

CANDLESTICK POINT PARK

San Francisco, California, 1985–93

Using the dominant forces of wind and water, Hargreaves refreshed the derelict Candlestick Point by shaping the land in its relationship to San Francisco Bay.

CRISSY FIELD

San Francisco, California, 1998–2000

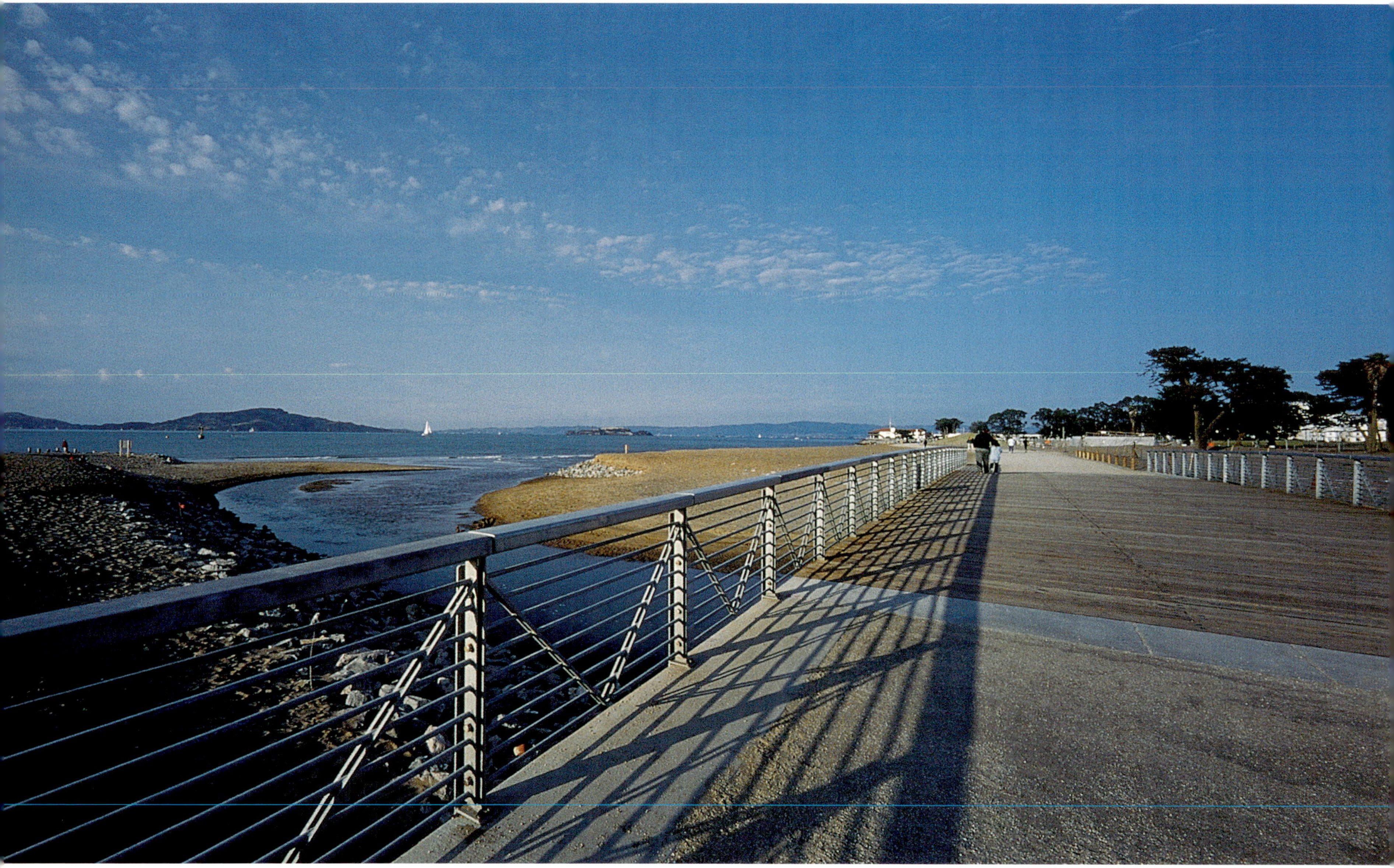

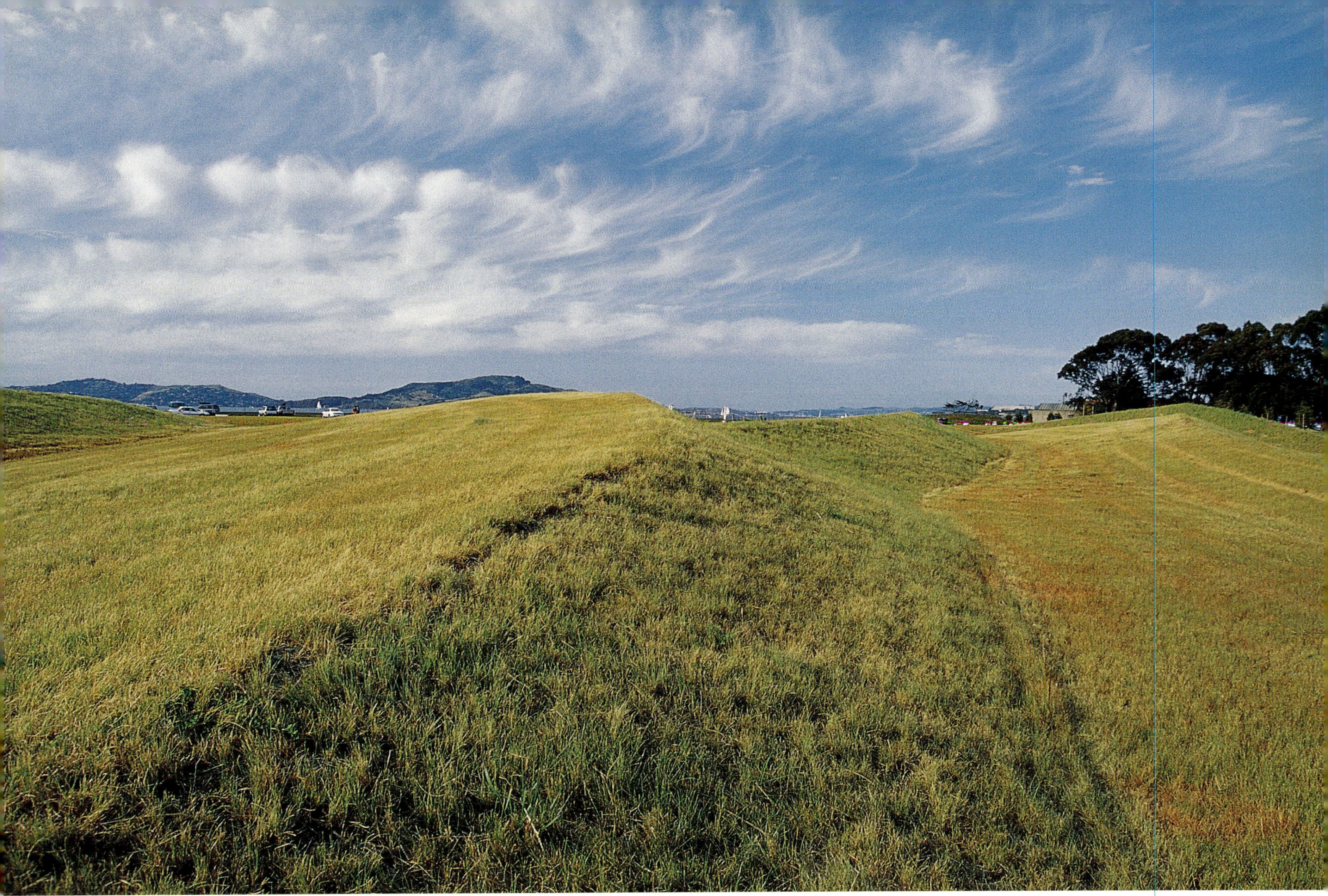

In the conversion of the historic airfield and military installation at Crissy Field to a multiuse park area, Hargreaves Associates created a landscape of wetlands, dune fields, and viewing points along the San Francisco Bay waterfront.

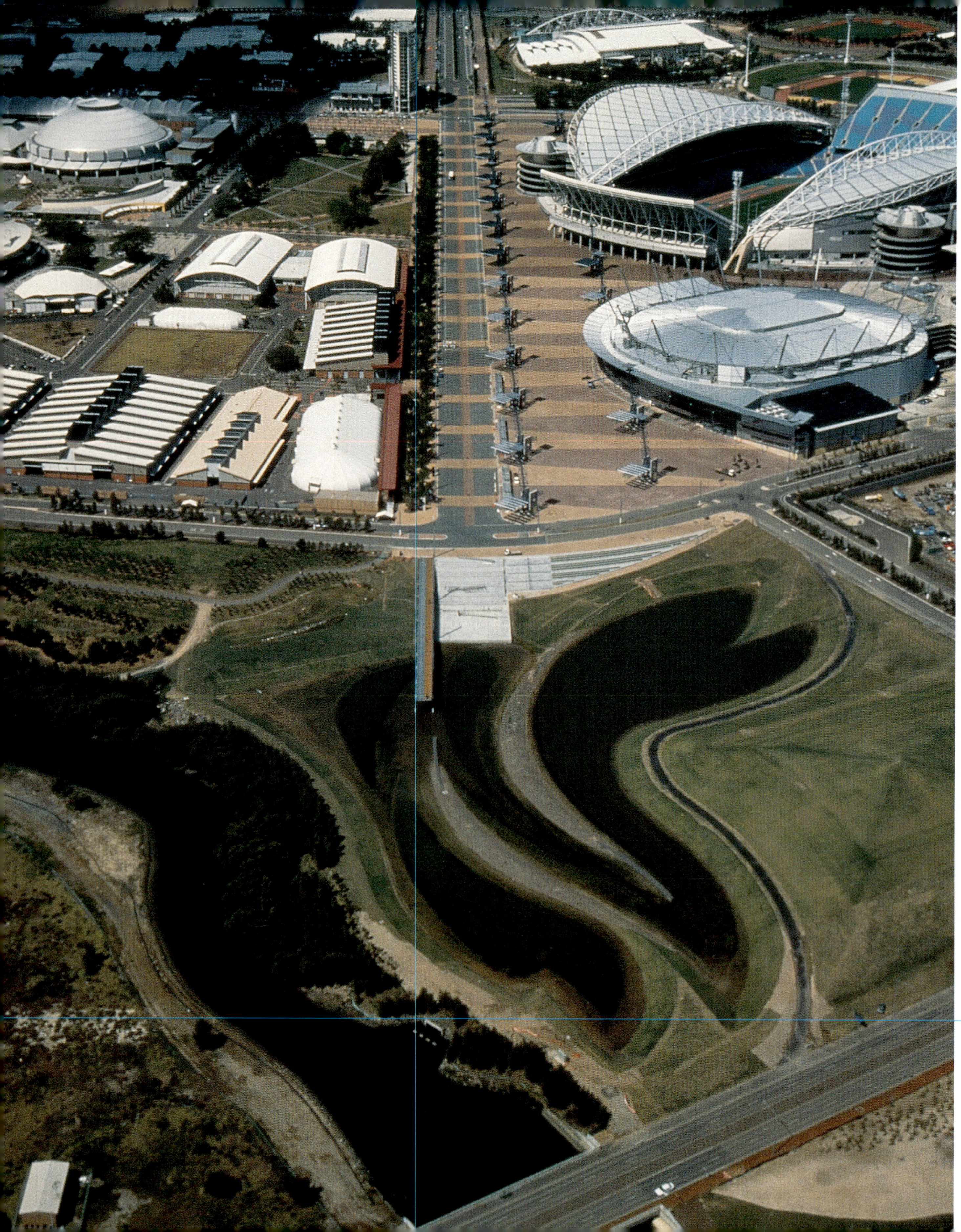

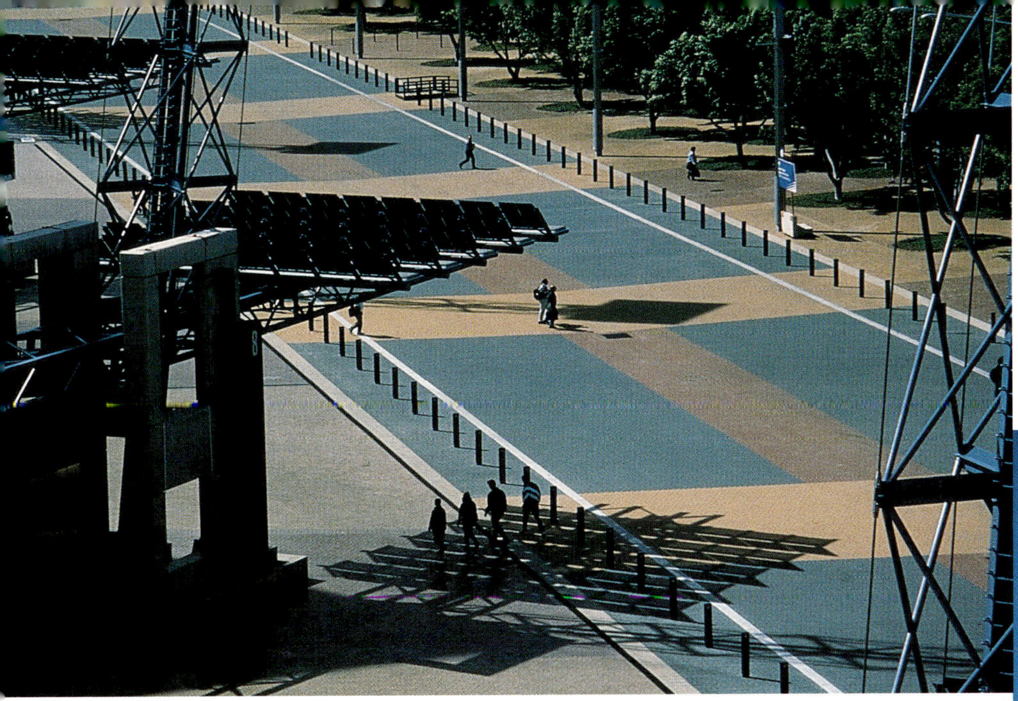

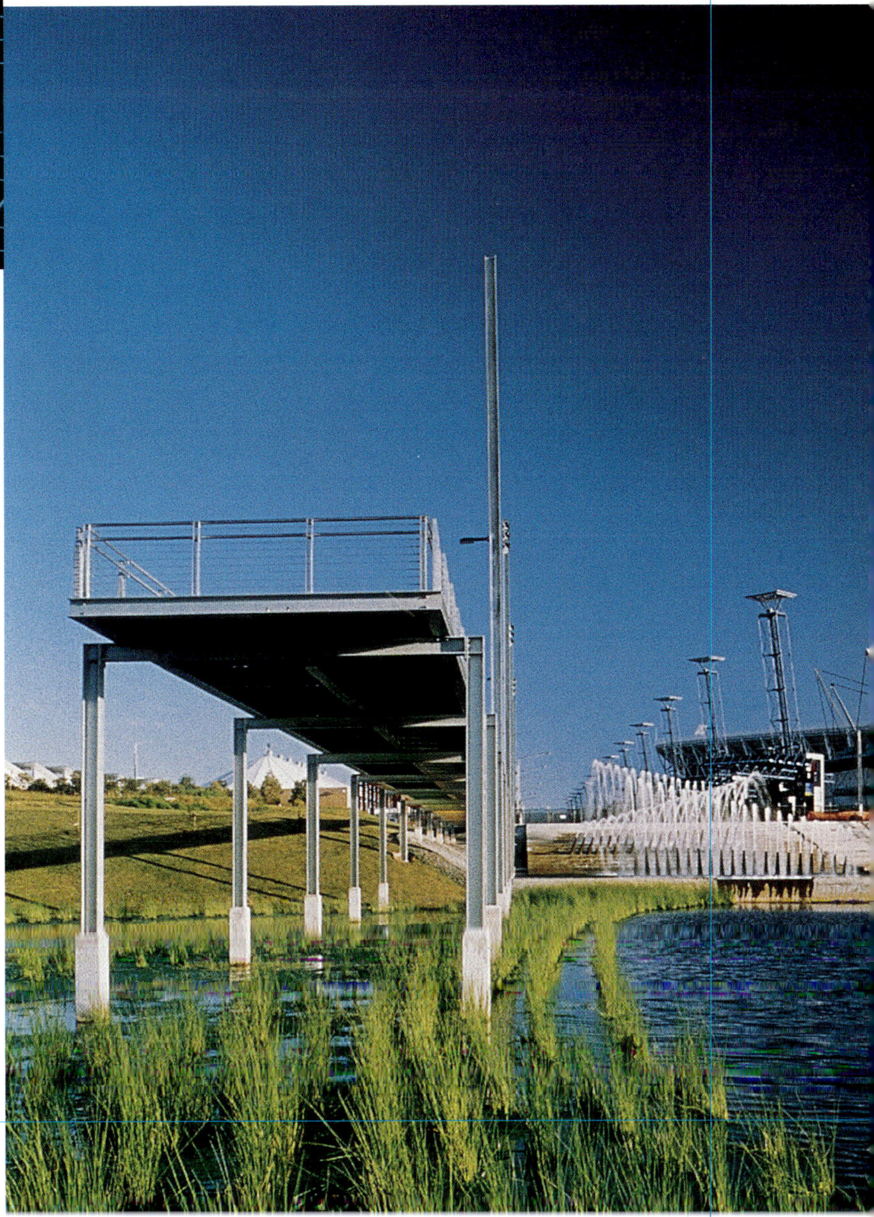

SYDNEY OLYMPIC PARK

Sydney, Australia, 1996–2000

For the 2000 Sydney Olympics, Hargreaves Associates created a park at the heart of Homebush Bay. The twenty-three-acre site served as the largest public gathering spot at the games and gave a sense of enlivened identity to the space.

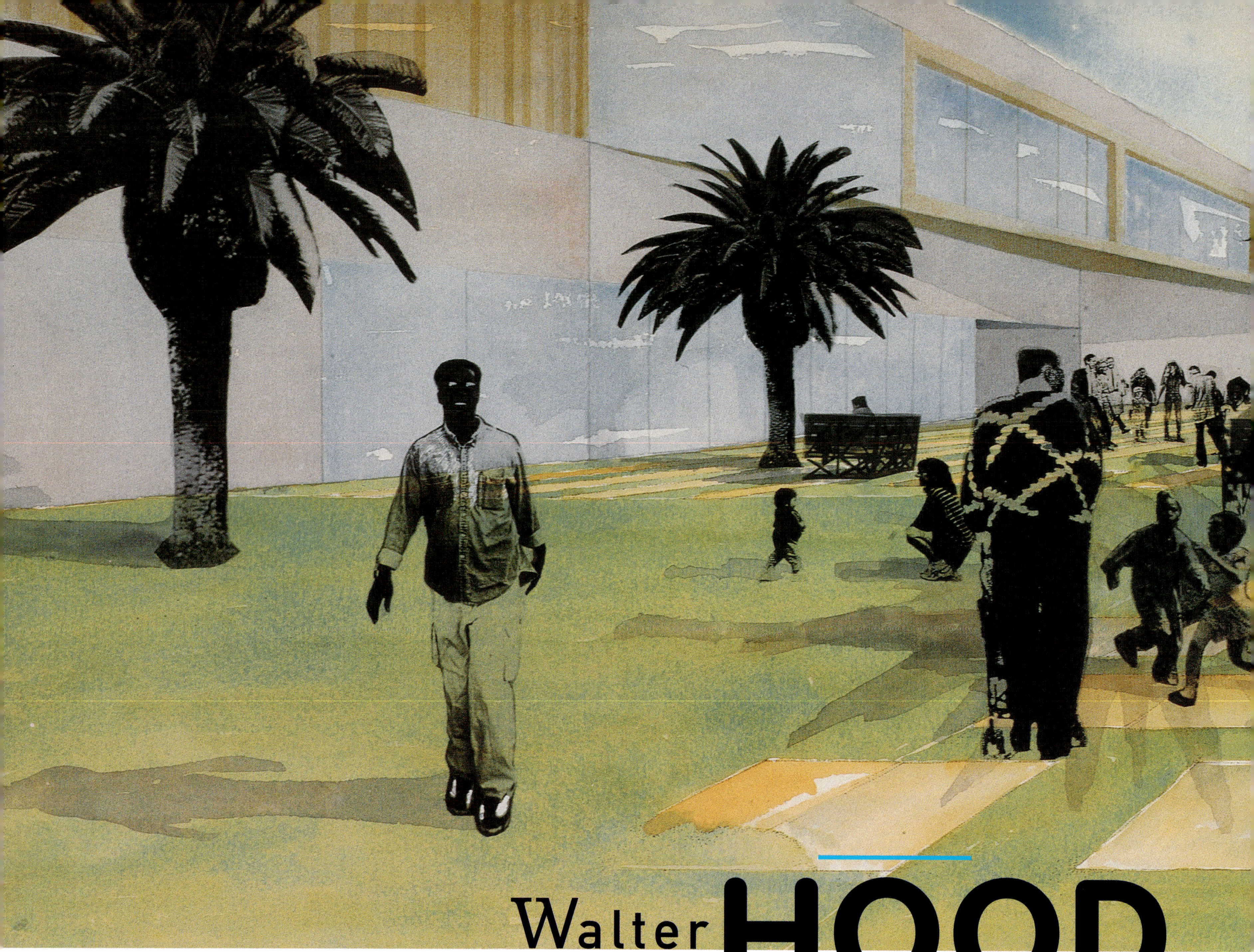

Walter HOOD

Gardens and Courts
M. H. DE YOUNG MEMORIAL MUSEUM

San Francisco, California, 2000
[front view]

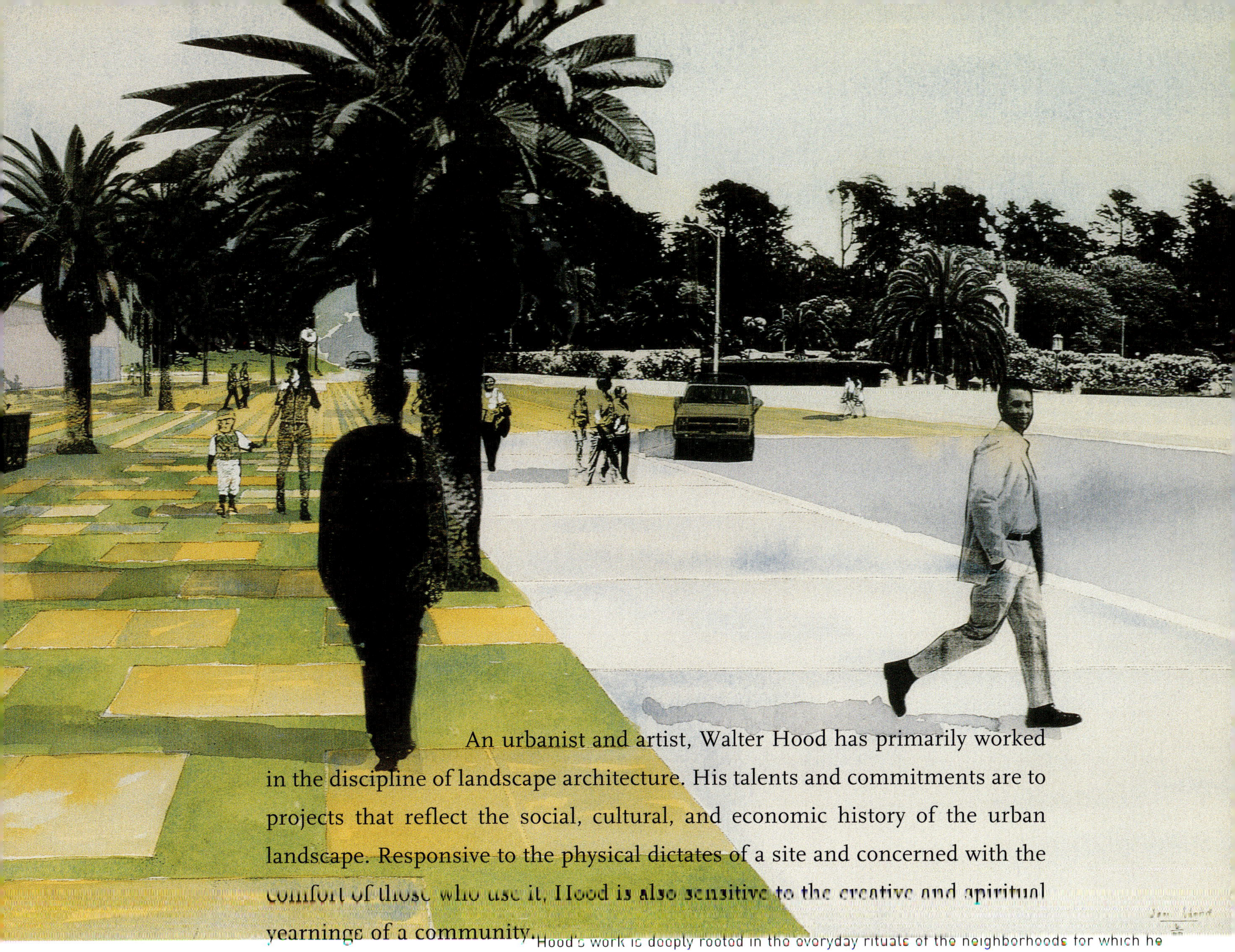

An urbanist and artist, Walter Hood has primarily worked in the discipline of landscape architecture. His talents and commitments are to projects that reflect the social, cultural, and economic history of the urban landscape. Responsive to the physical dictates of a site and concerned with the comfort of those who use it, Hood is also sensitive to the creative and spiritual yearnings of a community.

Hood's work is deeply rooted in the everyday rituals of the neighborhoods for which he designs. His first built projects were modest parks in Oakland, California, where he lives and works. While engaged in making real parks, he also imagined other parks for that community. His book, *Urban Diaries*, includes ideas for parks, with barbecues for homeless urban picnickers and spaces for shopping-cart recyclers, structures for driveway merchants, and even a system of drive-in brothels. Like his built work, these theoretical projects evolved from what Hood calls an improvisational approach, transpositions of spontaneous change within a traditional design framework. Over time, he carefully observes the uses and circumstances of a site, and then, imposing as few preconceived notions as possible, he searches for creative solutions.

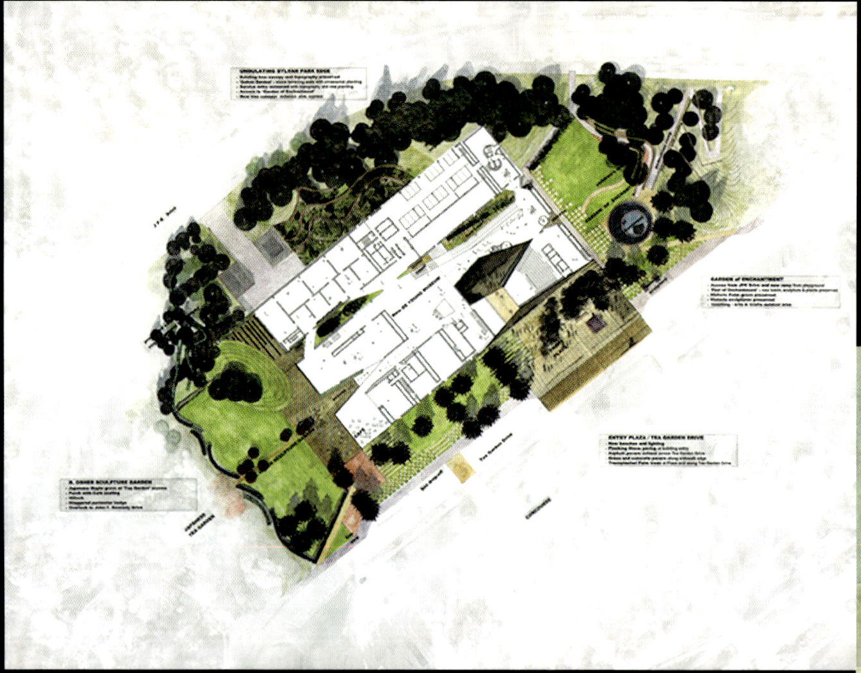

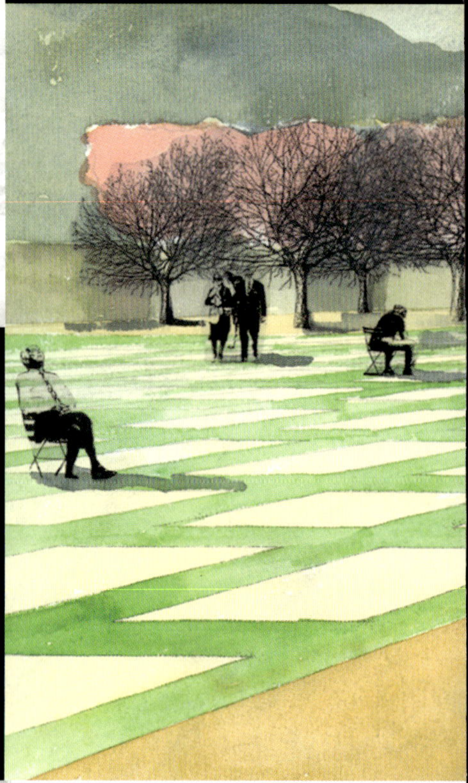

Gardens and Courts
M. H. DE YOUNG MEMORIAL MUSEUM

San Francisco, California, 2000

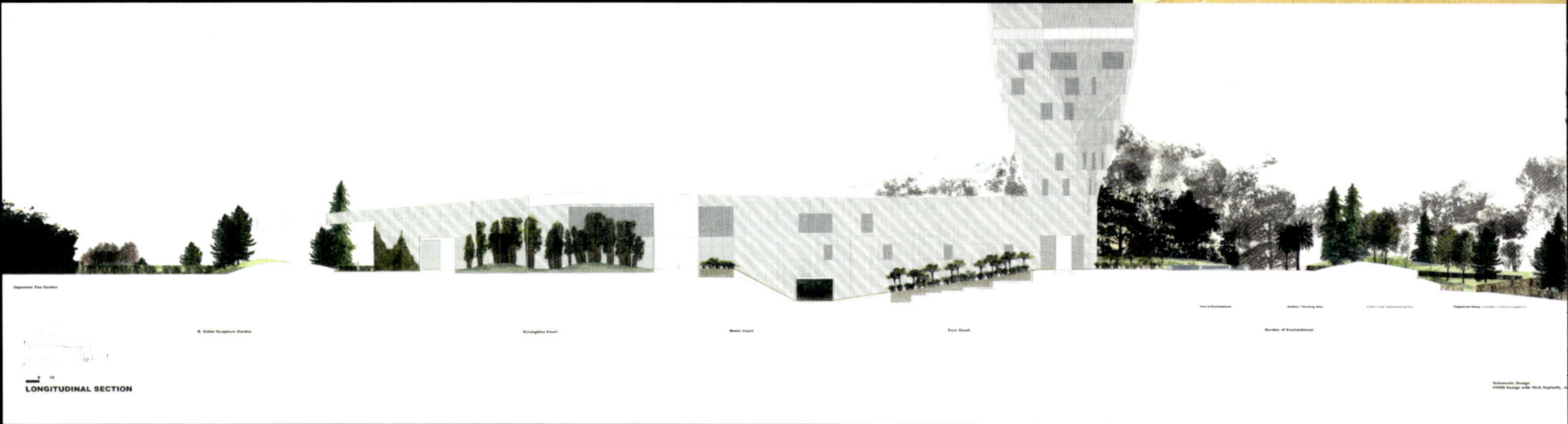

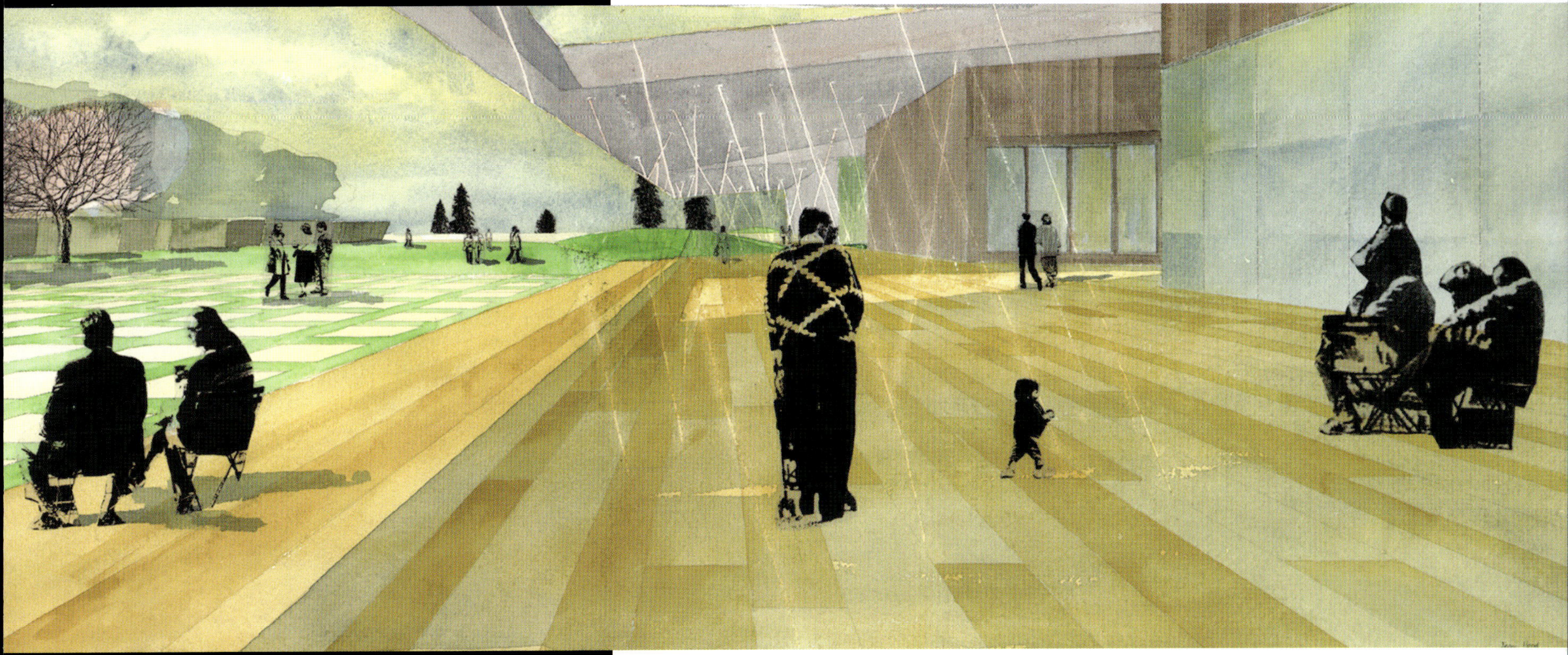

Hood's landscape plan for the new M. H. de Young Memorial Museum to be built in Golden Gate Park recognizes the extraordinary array of plants in the great park by placing examples of them in the new gardens surrounding the museum, making the beauty of the park more accessible to museum goers.

Oakland, California 1994–2001

LAFAYETTE SQUARE PARK

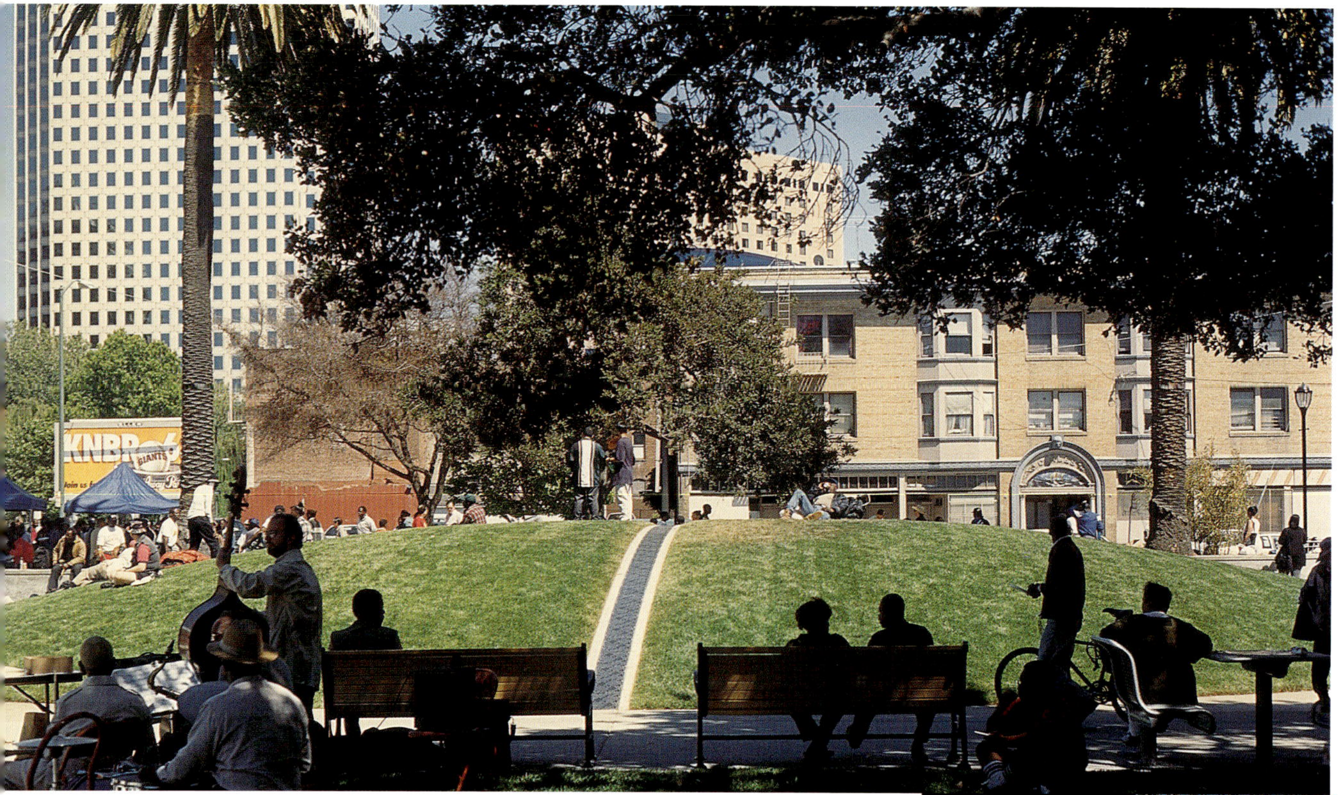

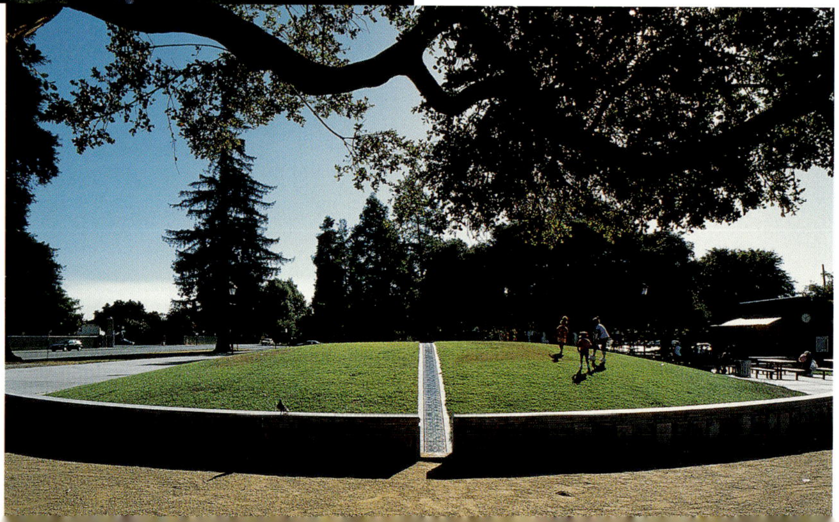

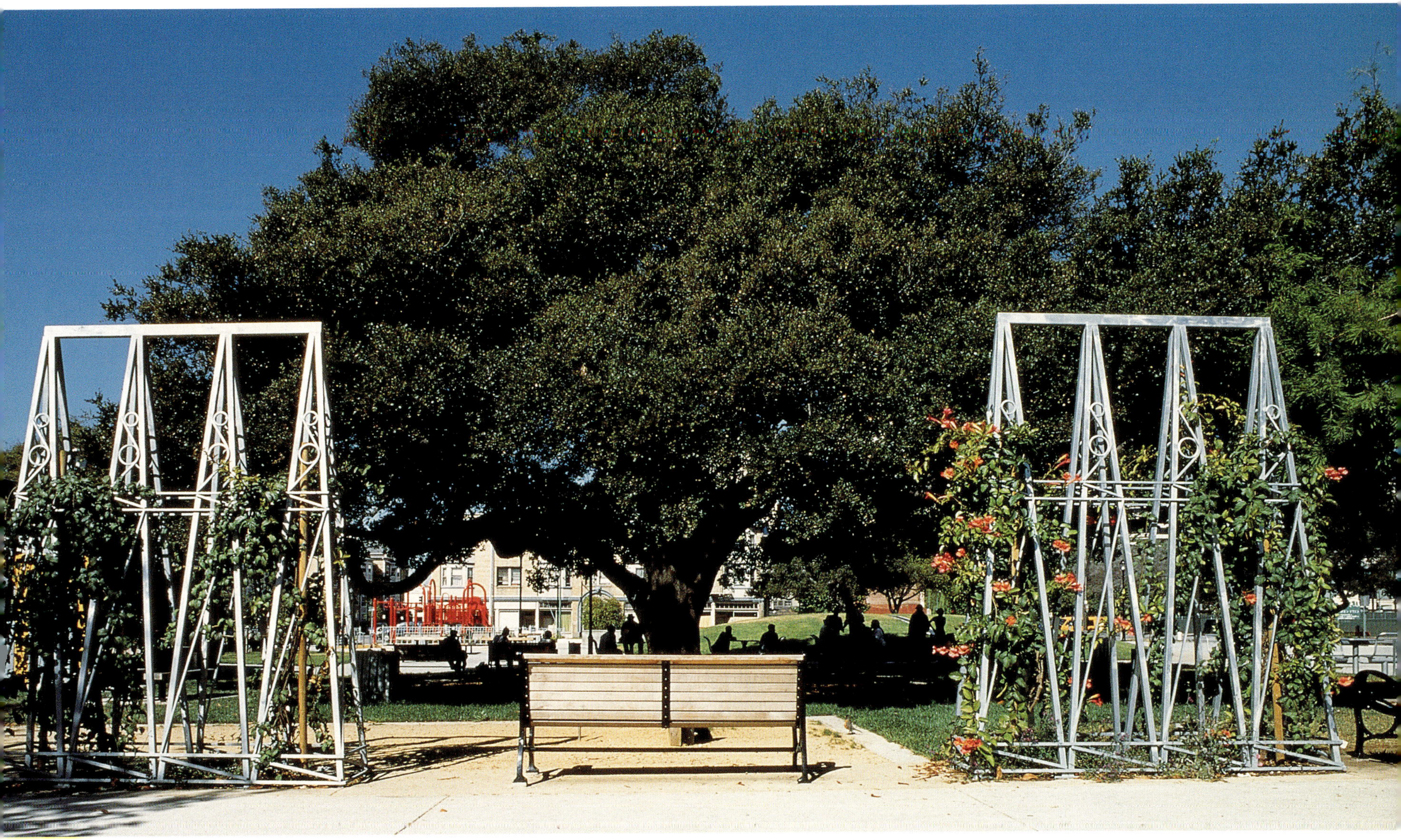

Located in a previously undeveloped site in downtown Oakland, Lafayette Square Park is a hybrid of park and city square. A central grass hillock holding an underground fountain is surrounded by play equipment, restrooms, barbeque facilities, and places to relax and linger.

POPLAR STREET IMPROVEMENT PROJECT

Macon, Georgia, 1998

For this project, Hood proposed "a scheme that builds on the life of the street." Echoing former use patterns of the community, Hood's respectful and fresh plan regenerated interest in the ailing neighborhood.

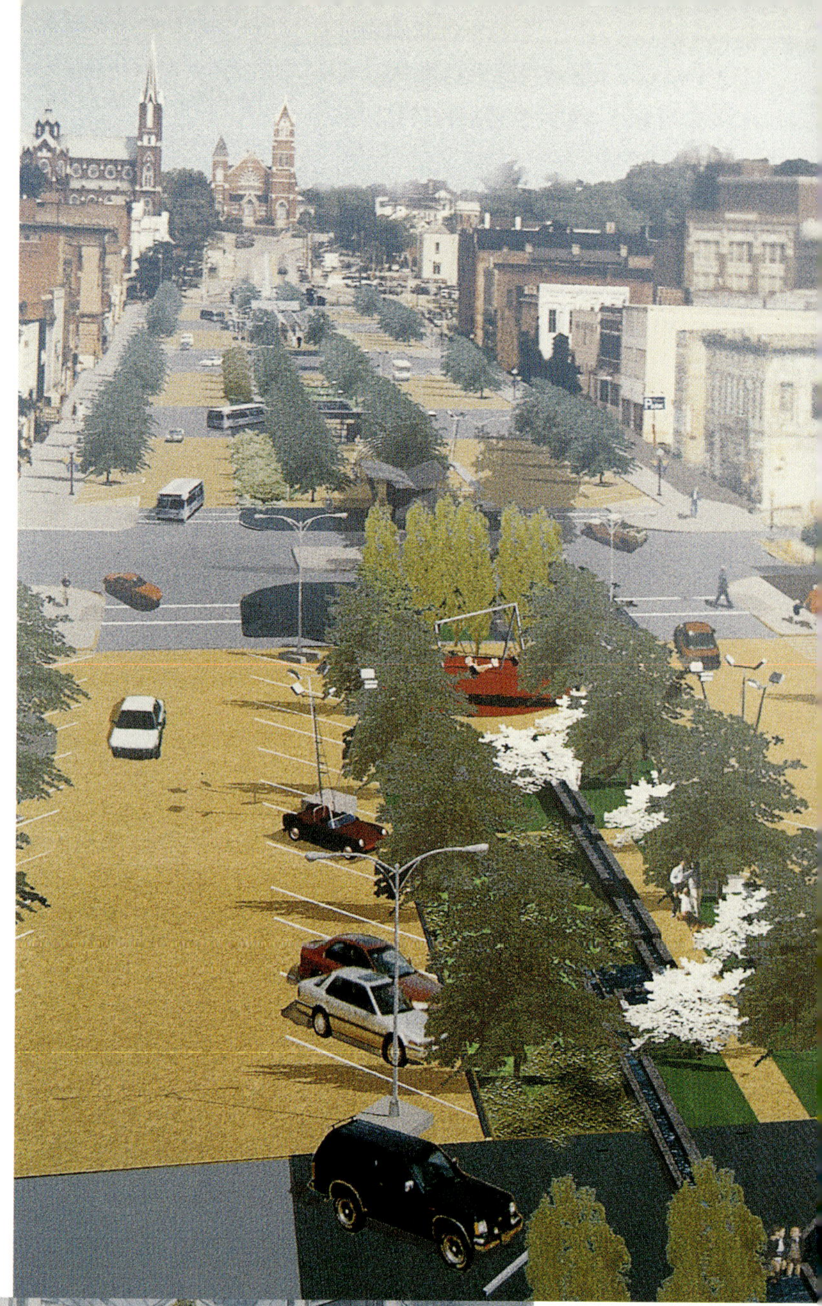

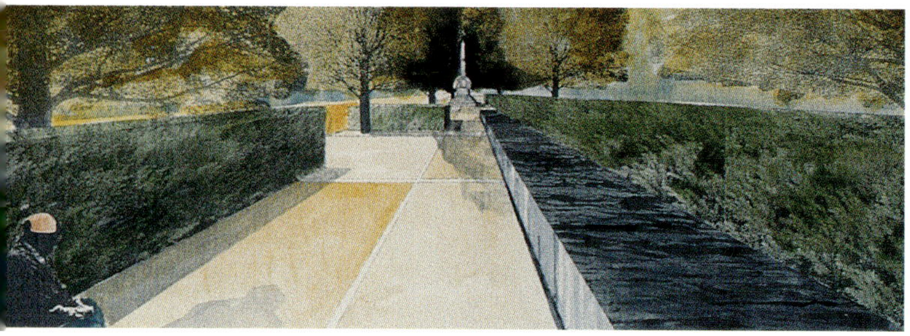

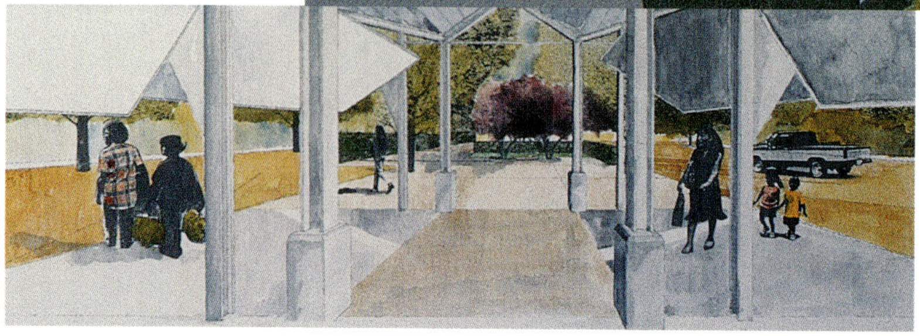

YERBA BUENA LANE

Hood Design and the Office of Cheryl Barton

San Francisco, California, 2001

Hood collaborated with landscape architect Cheryl Barton to orchestrate a unique mid-block walkway connecting the heart of downtown San Francisco with Yerba Buena Gardens.

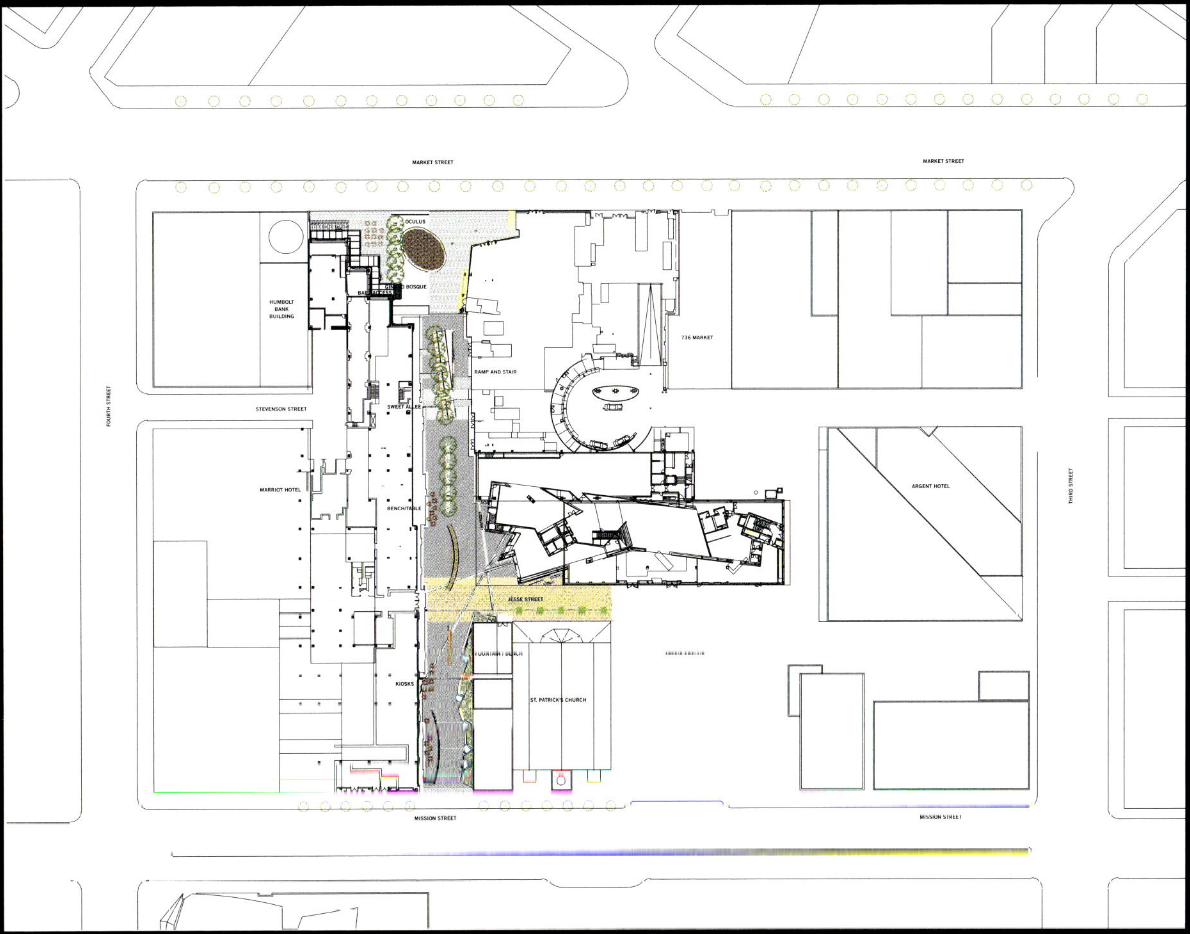

Tom Leader's work is inspired by open inquiry and the interrelationship of underlying systems that range from the connection between the human body and the landscape to that between surface layers and excavated meaning. His concern is always for the element of discovery in the process. Approaching particular sites as segments of a greater geology marked by specific and universal systems of all kinds, his work traces movement through the landscape and produces a record of that encounter.

Formerly a partner, for fifteen years, in the firm of Peter Walker and Partners, Leader was head designer on projects in locations as wide ranging as Japan and Washington State. His work has also evolved from his own investigations and observations, many focused on sites in the San Francisco Bay Area, where Leader envisions the landscape as having a consistent seriality. His designs assess and reveal the landscape in its varied layers, cuts, sections, interruptions, and interventions. While taking inspiration from the macrocosm, Leader's work ends up "on the ground," making a place for the individual's physical marking of time; each layer of geology in a process of evolution, for instance, is analogous to the repeated human step. Among the influences on his work are minimalism and Zen Buddhism, both of which find meaning and expression in the value of a repeated gesture.

inspired by open inquiry and the interrelationship of underlying systems

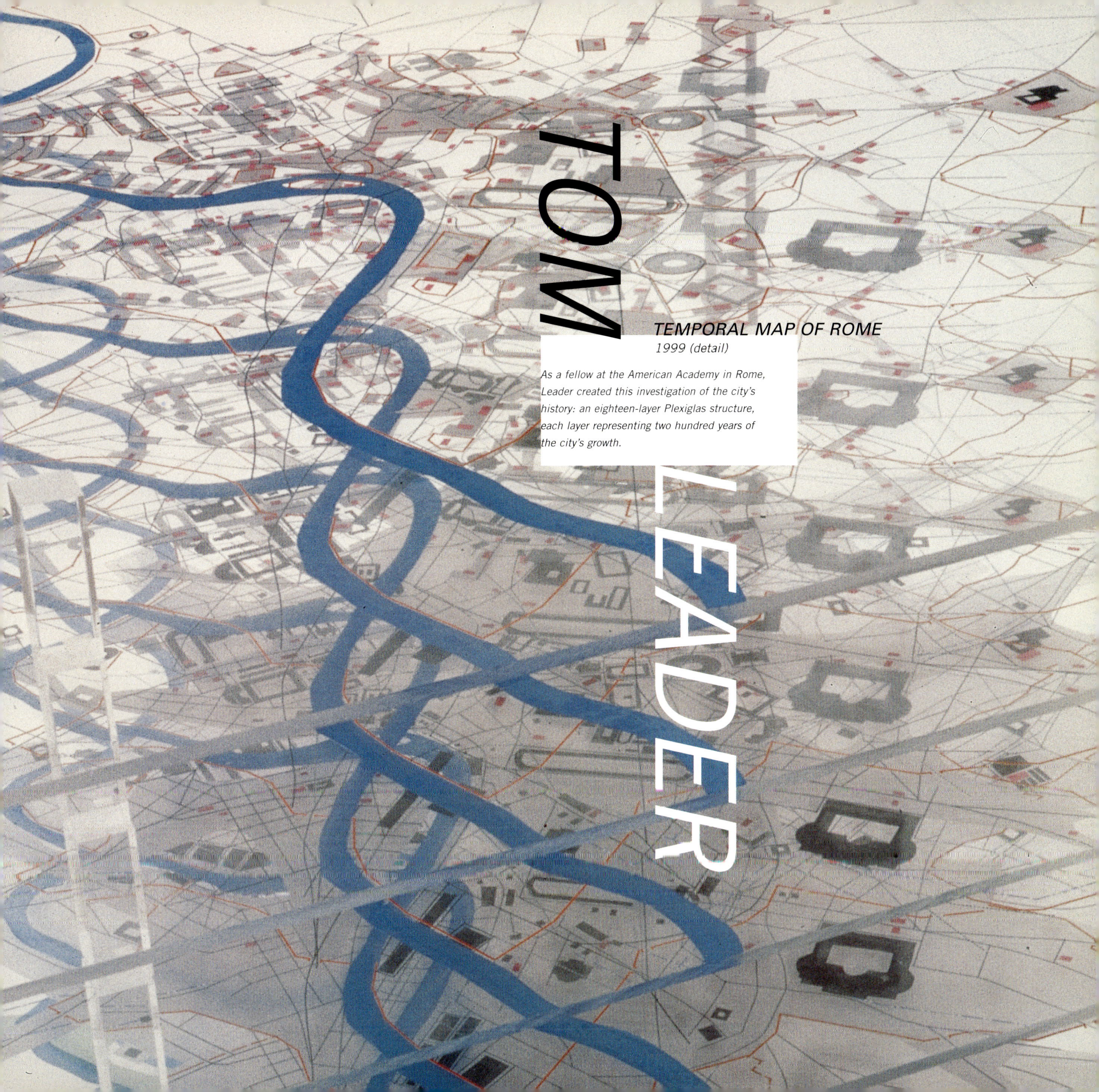

TOM LEADER

TEMPORAL MAP OF ROME
1999 (detail)

As a fellow at the American Academy in Rome, Leader created this investigation of the city's history: an eighteen-layer Plexiglas structure, each layer representing two hundred years of the city's growth.

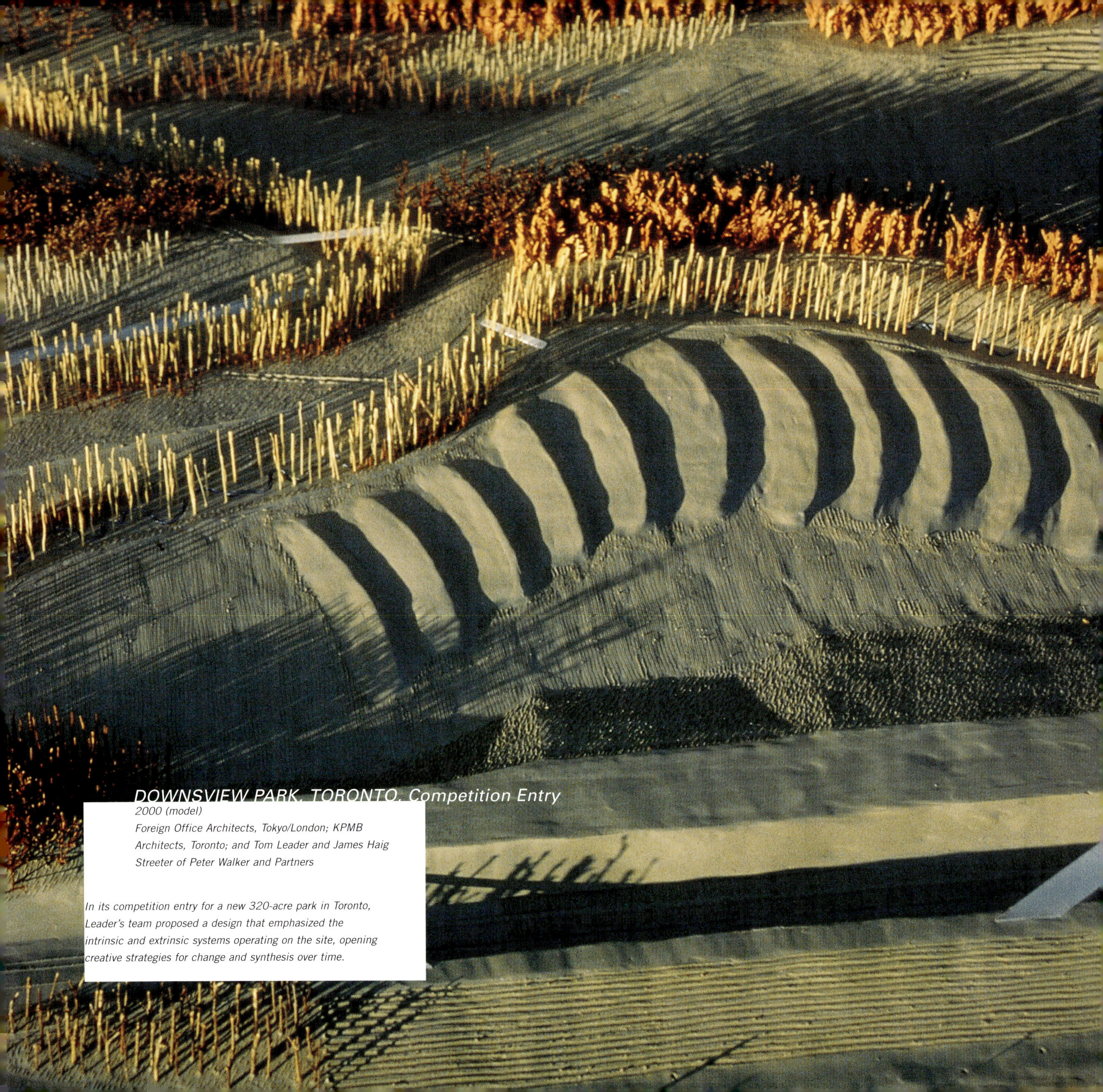

DOWNSVIEW PARK, TORONTO, Competition Entry
2000 (model)
Foreign Office Architects, Tokyo/London; KPMB Architects, Toronto; and Tom Leader and James Haig Streeter of Peter Walker and Partners

In its competition entry for a new 320-acre park in Toronto, Leader's team proposed a design that emphasized the intrinsic and extrinsic systems operating on the site, opening creative strategies for change and synthesis over time.

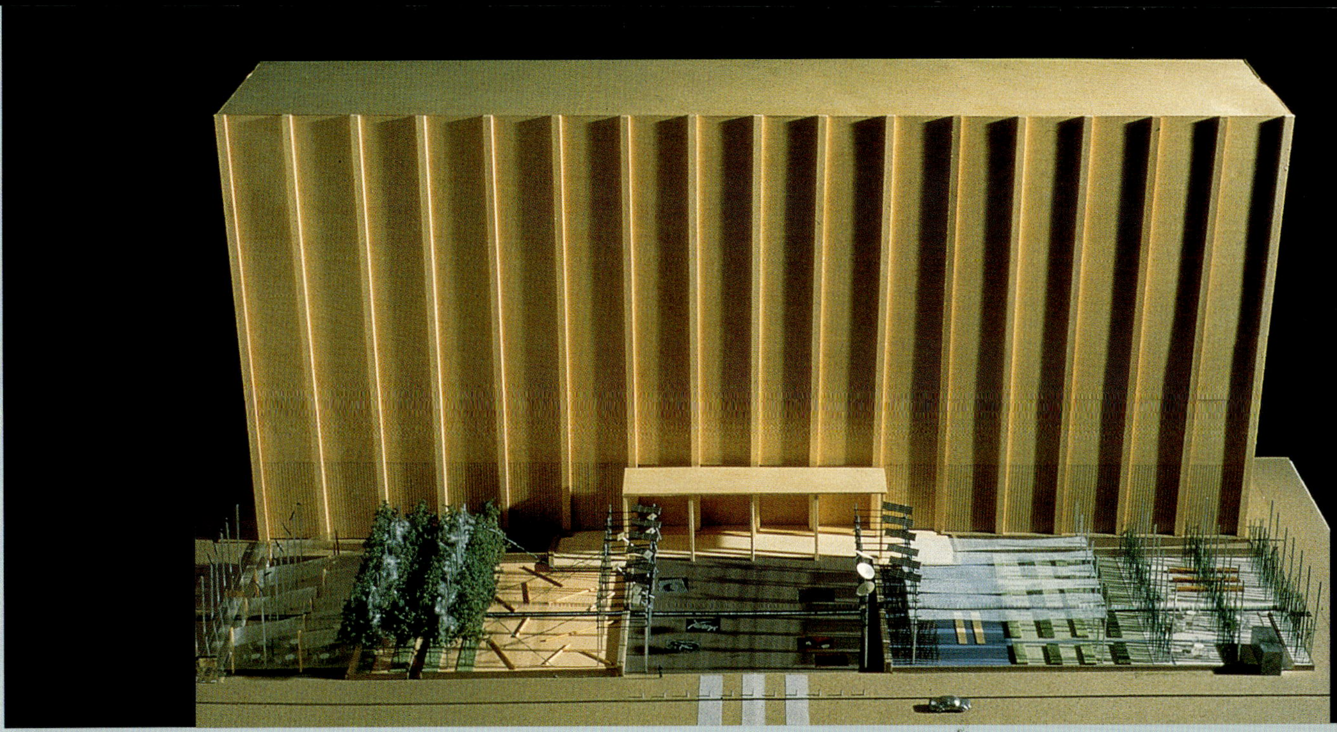

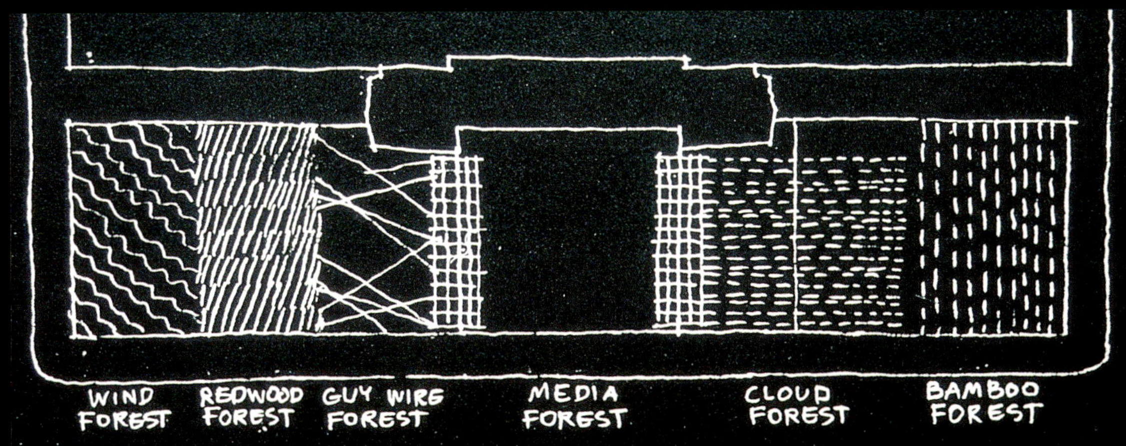

DEMONSTRATION FOREST

Phillip Burton Federal Building Plaza (Competition Entry for 1996 San Francisco Prize), 1996 (model and plan)

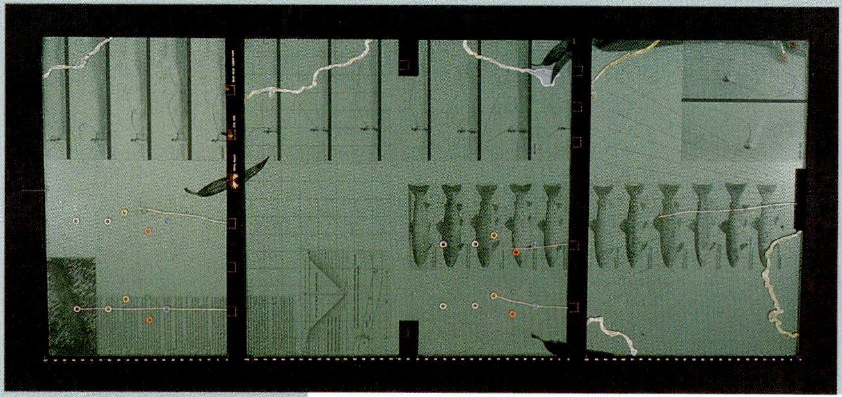

As one of a series of projects referencing sites that influenced his way of seeing and his work, Leader created a collaged map of a flycasting pond in Golden Gate Park, emphasizing the reflections he saw in the sequences of ripples, shadows, and repeated motions of the fishermen.

FLYCASTING PONDS, GOLDEN GATE PARK

1996

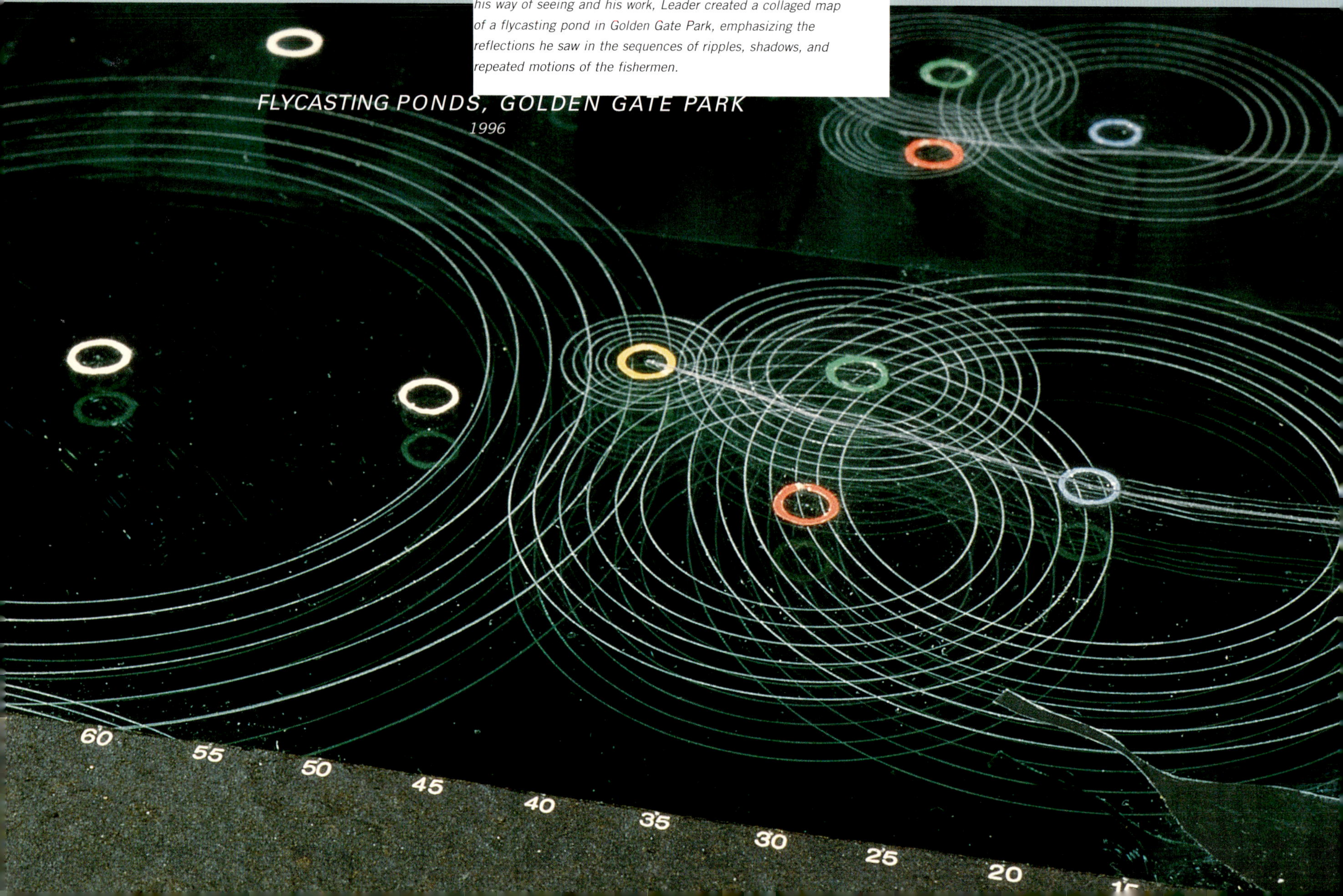

CONTAINER TRANSFER TERMINAL, PORT OF OAKLAND

1996

As part of his research into the patterns of vernacular landscapes, Leader created this collaged map of the movement and storage of large shipping containers at the Port of Oakland.

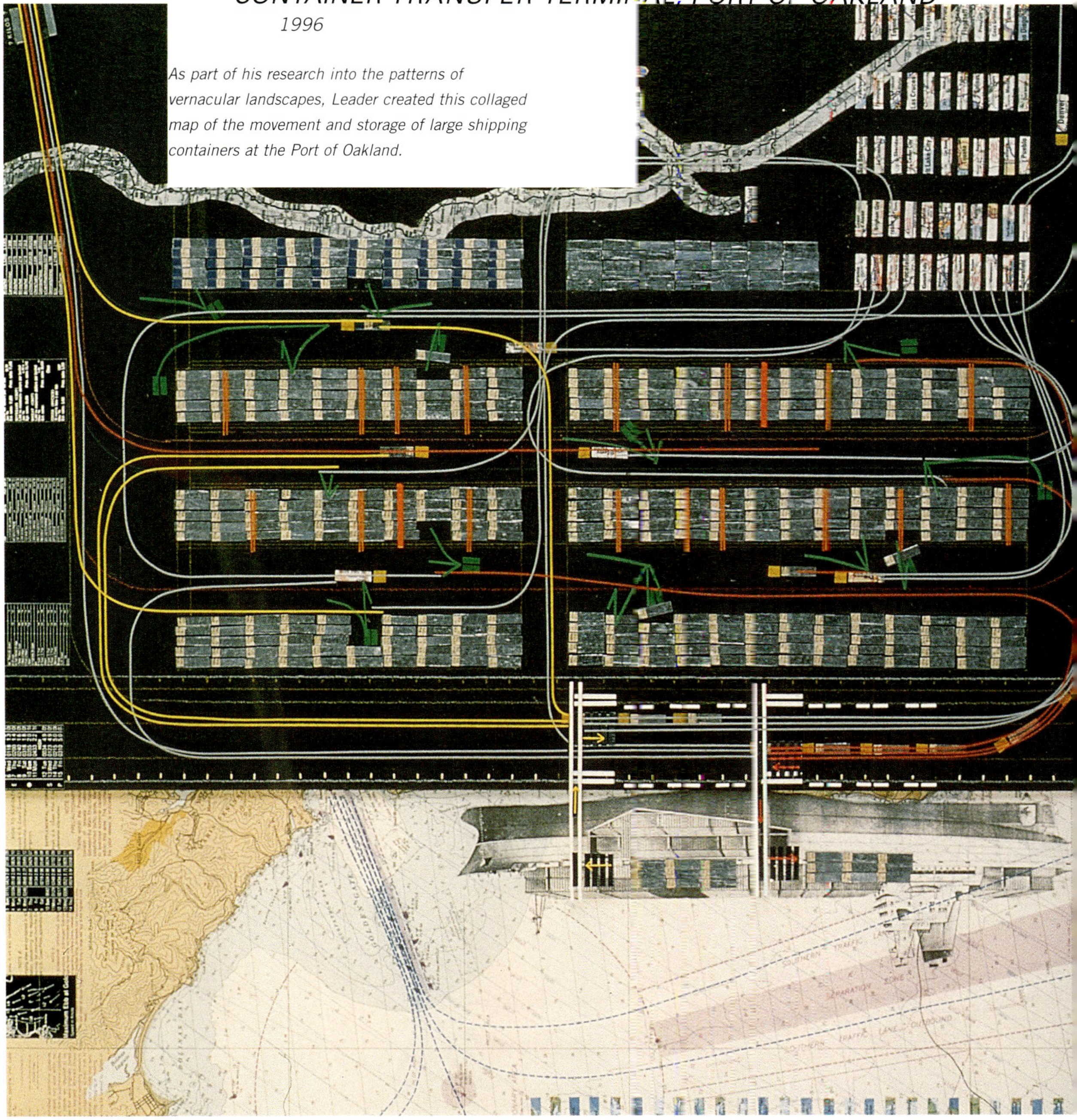

LONGACRES PARK

Renton, Washington, 1993

Tom Leader for Peter Walker and Partners

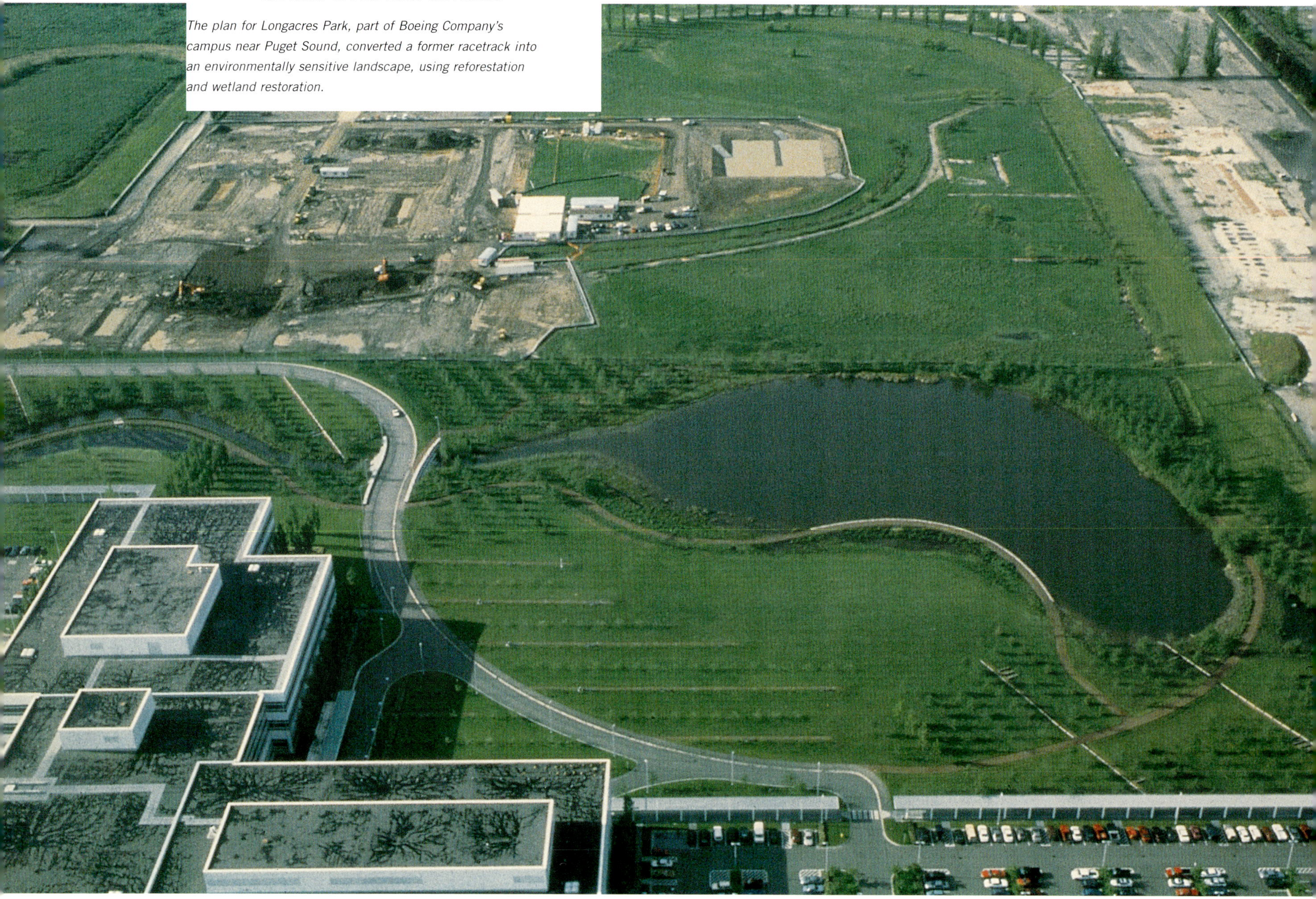

The plan for Longacres Park, part of Boeing Company's campus near Puget Sound, converted a former racetrack into an environmentally sensitive landscape, using reforestation and wetland restoration.

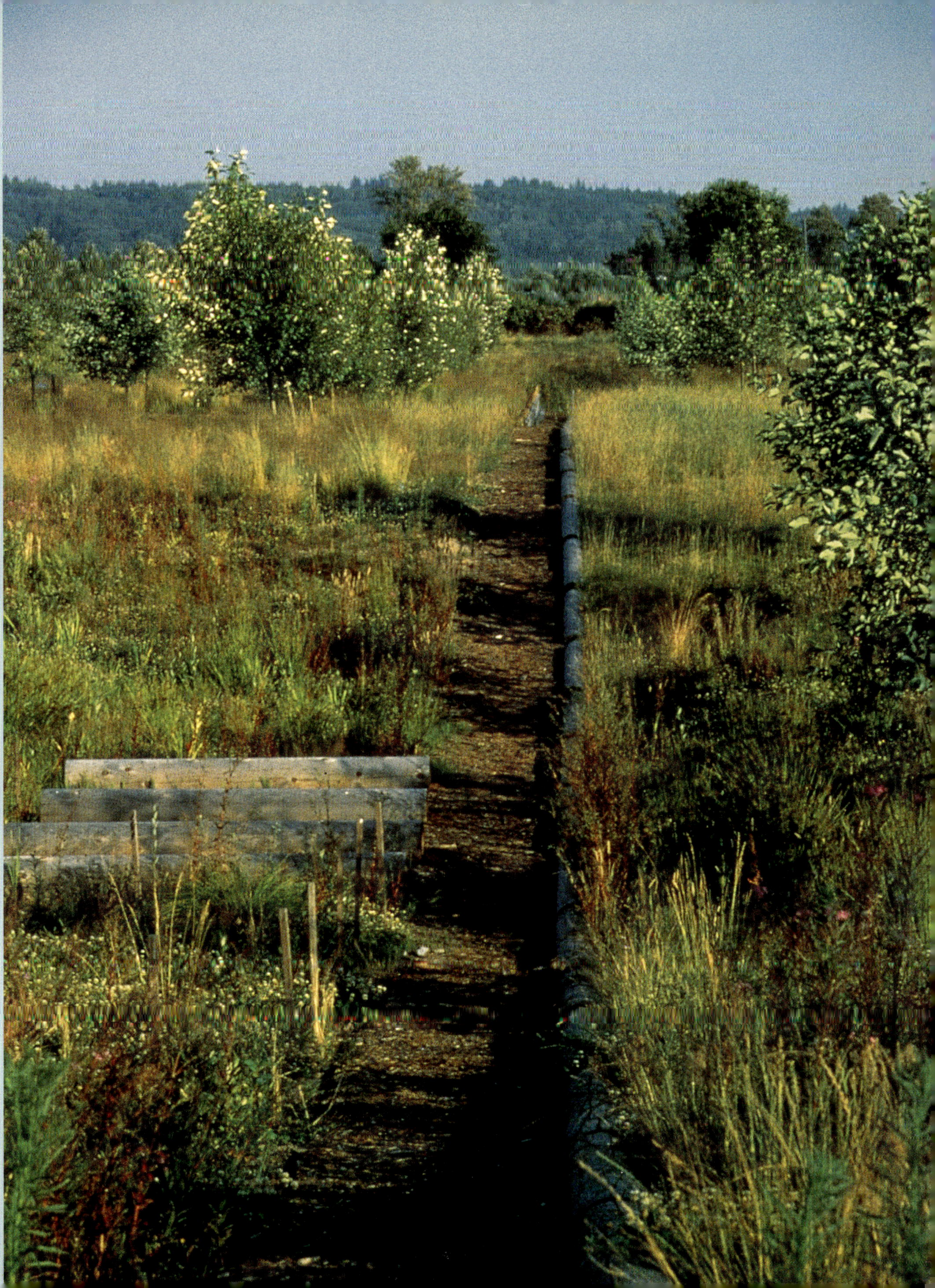

Kathryn Gustafson, Jaimi Baer +
Conger Moss Guillard Landscape Architecture

Biographies

Kathryn Gustafson is an environmental artist and landscape designer who now makes her home on Vashon Island in Washington. She has been designing gardens, parks, plazas, and community spaces for twenty years. Gustafson began her career in fashion, graduating from New York's Fashion Institute of Technology in 1971, and went on to earn a degree in landscape architecture at the Ecole Nationale Supérieure du Paysage in Versailles in 1979. Her landscape designs, with their flowing, unfolding surfaces and their attention to texture and formal detail, continue to reflect her early interest in textiles. Among her best-known projects are the redesign of park landscaping for the Crystal Palace, London, in 1996; the design of a park and garden in Terrasson, France, in 1995; and the design of the grounds for the French headquarters of Shell Petroleum, in Rueil-Malmaison, in 1991.

Architect Jaimi Baer, a San Francisco native who works in San Rafael, California, has specialized in civic and community projects for the past ten years. Her work focuses on how space is perceived through the use of light and color. Baer frequently collaborates with artists on her projects, overseeing the incorporation of their work into the architectural program. She first worked with Kathryn Gustafson in 1994 on a design proposal for the San Francisco International Airport. While completing adaptive re-use projects at Headlands Center for the Arts, Baer was introduced to many artists whose work is informed by a sense of place, with whom she continues to work.

The San Francisco firm of Conger Moss Guillard Landscape Architecture (CMG) was founded in 2000 to pursue projects that explore the conceptualization and cultivation of the urban landscape. CMG's three founding partners, Kevin Conger, Willett Moss, and Chris Guillard, share an enthusiasm for working within collaborative alliances, believing that the cross-pollination of ideas fosters the most innovative responses to the complex challenges inherent in contemporary landscape projects.

Hargreaves Associates
in collaboration with **Julian Lang**

George Hargreaves is the founder and design director of Hargreaves Associates, based in San Francisco and Cambridge, Mass. He is also a tenured professor of landscape architecture and the chairman of the Department of Landscape Architecture at the Harvard University Graduate School of Design, where he has taught since 1986. He received his M.L.A. (Master of Landscape Architecture) degree from Harvard in 1979.

Mary Margaret Jones is president of Hargreaves Associates. She is a fellow of the American Academy in Rome and has been a visiting critic at Harvard's Graduate School of Design. She received a bachelor's degree in landscape architecture from Texas A&M University's College of Architecture and Environmental Design in 1979.

The firm's award-winning projects include the master concept design for the Sydney Olympics 2000, the University of Cincinnati master plan, Byxbee Park in Palo Alto, and Crissy Field in San Francisco's Presidio. One of the firm's signature projects is the Guadalupe River Park in San Jose, a series of landscaped public spaces aligning three miles of the Guadalupe River running through the metropolitan area. Begun in 1986, the project integrates flood control with recreation spaces and a wild-life habitat. The design, in its sensitivity to natural systems combined with a reliance on sophisticated engineering, is typical of the firm's approach.

Writer and teacher Julian Lang founded the Institute of Native Knowledge in 1989 to preserve and promote the culture of California's indigenous populations. Lang is currently teaching the Karuk language, native to northern California, to a group of performers who plan to resurrect the tribe's traditional ceremonies. With the aid of tribal elders, he is also compiling an encyclopedia of Karuk knowledge. A frequent speaker at universities throughout California, Lang is a guest columnist for *Artweek* and writes for Berkeley's *News From Native California* on native music, political developments impacting native communities and religions, the appropriation of native intellectual properties, and material culture.

Hood Design in collaboration with
Olly Wilson + Douglas Hollis

Walter Hood has been a professor in the Department of Landscape Architecture at the University of California at Berkeley since 1990. He founded Hood Design in Oakland in 1993, and his work includes housing projects, private residences, and public parks, among them Lafayette Square in downtown Oakland. Hood is the landscape architect for the new M. H. de Young Memorial Museum to be built in San Francisco and a member of the design team for Yerba Buena Lane, a new pedestrian pathway in downtown San Francisco. He makes his home in West Oakland. The neighborhood's dual identity—once the very heart of a thriving African American culture in the East Bay and now an eroded area—inspires much of Hood's writings on urban planning. "Improvisation" is his term for flexibility in urban planning—the ability of a design to respond dynamically to specific and unique needs in a neighborhood instead of applying a generic or theoretical approach. Hood's experimental designs have been exhibited at the Berkeley Art Museum and the Walker Art Center in Minneapolis.

A native of St. Louis, composer Olly Wilson has been a professor of music at the University of California at Berkeley for thirty years. He is the recipient of two Guggenheim fellowships and two National Endowment for the Arts commissions. His compositions, including works for chamber ensembles, orchestras, and electronic media, have been performed by the New York Philharmonic and the Moscow Philharmonic, as well as the symphony orchestras of Boston, Chicago, San Francisco, and many other cities. Wilson spent two years living and studying music in West Africa and has published scholarly articles on African and African American music.

Douglas Hollis is an artist whose outdoor, site-specific installations are designed to interact with wind, water, temperature, and other natural phenomena. His works include *A Sound Garden*, installed at the National Oceanic and Atmospheric Administration in Seattle, and *Rain Column*, at the Rincon Center in San Francisco. Hollis, who received his B.F.A. degree from the University of Michigan in 1970, has previously collaborated with a number of artists, architects, and landscape architects, including George Hargreaves, Adèle Naude Santos, and Mark Mack.

Tom Leader Studio in collaboration with
Anuradha Mathur + Dilip da Cunha

Tom Leader is founder and principal of Tom Leader Studio in Berkeley, California. Previously he was a partner in the Berkeley firm of Peter Walker and Partners, where he was manager for two award-winning projects: Longacres Park near Seattle and Asahikawa River Park on the island of Hokkaido, Japan. Leader has also pursued more speculative research into engineered landscapes untouched by design, such as container ports, produce farms, and fly-casting pools. Map constructions resulting from these investigations have been acquired by the San Francisco Museum of Modern Art for its permanent collection. A California native, Leader received his M.L.A. degree from the Harvard University Graduate School of Design in 1983. In 1996 he was a winner of the San Francisco Prize Competition for the design of the plaza at the Phillip Burton Federal Building, and in 1998 he won the Rome Prize in landscape architecture at the American Academy in Rome. Leader is founder and editor of Juncus.com, a Web site dedicated to critical exchange in landscape architecture.

Anuradha Mathur has been an assistant professor of landscape architecture and regional planning at the University of Pennsylvania since 1994. After earning a bachelor's degree in architecture at the School of Architecture, Ahmedabad, India, in 1986, she received her M.L.A. degree from the University of Pennsylvania in 1991. Her recent work, an exhibition on the lower Mississippi River landscape titled *Mississippi Horizons: Mapping a Shifting Terrain*, has traveled in the United States and Europe.

Dilip da Cunha is a lecturer at the University of Pennsylvania and at the Parsons School of Design in New York. He is an architect who received a master's degree in city planning from the Massachusetts Institute of Technology in 1989 and a Ph.D. in city and regional planning from the University of California at Berkeley in 1996. With collaborator Anuradha Mathur, he has participated in a number of competitions that demand a reenvisioning of the public realm; these include the reuse of Governors Island in New York Harbor and the design of the Oklahoma Memorial in Oklahoma City.

Selected Bibliography

GENERAL

Beardsley, John. *Art and Landscape in Charleston and the Low Country: A Project of Spoleto Festival USA.* Washington, D.C.: Spacemaker Press, 1998.

Bourdon, David. *Designing the Earth: The Human Impulse to Shape Nature.* New York: Harry N. Abrams, Inc., 1995.

Brown, Brenda, ed. *Landscape Journal* (Special Issue: *Eco-Revelatory Design: Nature Constructed/Nature Revealed*) (1998).

Castells, Manuel. *The Information Age: Economy, Society and Culture.* Oxford, England: Blackwell Publishers, 1999.

Clay, Grady. *Real Places: An Unconventional Guide to America's Generic Landscape.* Chicago: University of Chicago Press, 1997.

Clifford, James. *Routes, Travel and Translation in the Late Twentieth Century.* Cambridge, Mass.: Harvard University Press, 1997.

Corner, James. "Eidetic Operations and New Landscapes." In *Recovering Landscape Architecture,* edited by James Corner. New York: Princeton Architectural Press, 1999.

Cronon, William, ed. *Uncommon Ground: Rethinking the Human Place in Nature.* New York: W. W. Norton & Co., Inc., 1995.

Dewey, John. *Art as Experience.* New York: Perigree Books, 1980.

Fagone, Vittorio, ed. *Art in Nature.* Milan, Italy: Edizioni Gabriele Mazzotta, 1996.

Hayden, Dolores. *The Power of Place: Urban Landscape as Public History.* Cambridge, Mass.: MIT Press, 1993.

Holt, Nancy, ed. *The Writings of Robert Smithson: Essays with Illustrations.* New York: New York University Press, 1979.

Jackson, John Brinckerhoff. *Landscape in Sight: Looking at America,* edited by Helen Lefkowitz Horowitz. New Haven: Yale University Press, 1997.

Jacob, Mary Jane. *Places with a Past: New Site-Specific Art at Charleston's Spoleto Festival.* New York: Rizzoli International Publications, 1991.

Kemal, Salim, and Ivan Gaskell, eds. *Landscape, Natural Beauty and the Arts.* Cambridge, England: Cambridge University Press, 1993.

Lerup, Lars. *After the City.* Cambridge, Mass.: MIT Press, 2000.

Lippard, Lucy R. *The Lure of the Local: Senses of Place in a Multicentered Society.* New York: The New Press, 1997.

———. *Overlay: Contemporary Art and the Art of Prehistory.* New York: Pantheon Books, 1983.

Lyall, Sutherland. *Designing the New Landscape.* London: Thames & Hudson, 1998.

Mitchell, William. *City of Bits: Space, Place and the Infobahn.* Cambridge, Mass.: MIT Press, 1995.

Morris, Robert. *Earthworks: Land Reclamation as Sculpture.* Seattle, Wash.: Seattle Art Museum, 1979.

Nye, David E. *American Technological Sublime.* Cambridge, Mass.: MIT Press, 1994.

Schama, Simon. *Landscape as Memory.* New York: Alfred A. Knopf, 1995.

Smith, Elizabeth A.T. et al. *Urban Revisions: Current Projects for the Public Realm.* Cambridge, Mass.: MIT Press/Museum of Contemporary Art, Los Angeles, 1994.

Soja, Edward W. "Reassertions: Towards a Spatial Ontology." In *Postmodern Geographies: The Reassertion of Space in Critical Social Theory.* London: Verso, 1989.

Sudjic, Deyan. *100 Mile City.* London: Harvest Books, 1993.

Treib, Marc, ed. *Modern Landscape Architecture: A Critical Review.* Cambridge, Mass.: MIT Press, 1993.

Walker, Peter, and Melanie Simo. *Invisible Gardens: The Search for Modernism in the American Landscape.* Cambridge, Mass.: MIT Press, 1994.

Weilacher, Udo. *Between Landscape Architecture and Land Art.* Trans. Felicity Goth. Basel: Birkhauser Verlag, 1999.

Weiss, Allen S. *Unnatural Horizons: Paradox and Contradiction in Landscape Architecture.* New York: Princeton Architectural Press, 1998.

Weyl, Martin, ed. *Hiriya in the Museum: Artists' and Architects' Proposals for Rehabilitation of the Site.* Tel Aviv, Israel: Tel Aviv Museum of Art, 1999.

Wright, Frank Lloyd. "The Art and Craft of the Machine." In *Frank Lloyd Wright: Writings and Buildings,* edited by Edgar Kaufman and Ben Raeburn. New York: New American Library, 1960.

Zapata, Christian. *The American Landscape.* New York: Princeton Architectural Press, 1995.

Zukin, Sharon. *Landscapes of Power from Detroit to Disney World.* Berkeley: University of California Press, 1991.

KATHRYN GUSTAFSON

Cooper, Guy, and Gordon Taylor. *Paradise Transformed: The Private Garden for the Twenty-First Century.* New York: Monacelli Press, 1996.

Diedrich, Lisa. "Kathryn Gustafson: Imagination and Form." *Topos. European Landscape Magazine,* no. 21 (December 1997): 16–26.

Holden, Robert, and Jennifer Hudson. *International Landscape Design.* London: Laurence King, 1996.

Levy, Leah. *Kathryn Gustafson: Sculpting the Land (The Land Marks Series, No. 5),* edited by Heidi Landecker. Washington, D.C.: Spacemaker Press, 1998.

Shepheard, Paul. "What Is Landscape?" *Blueprint,* no. 152 (July/August 1998): 20–24.

Uide, A. "Greenhouse Effect." *The Architectural Review* 203, no. 1215 (May 1998): 79–81.

Von Schaewen, Diedi. *Gardens in France.* Cologne: Taschen Publishing, 1997.

Young, Chris. "Expanding Horizons: Chris Young Talks to Kathryn Gustafson about Designing 'Anything with a Sky.'" *Landscape Design,* no. 277 (February 1999): 42–43.

HARGREAVES ASSOCIATES

Beardsley, John. *Earthworks and Beyond: Contemporary Art in the Landscape.* 3rd ed. New York: Abbeville Press, 1998.

———. "Poet of Landscape Process." *Landscape Architecture* 85 (December 1995): 46–51.

Bennett, Paul. "Big Ideas Down Under." *Landscape Architecture* 89, no. 2 (February 1999): 60–67.

———. "The Other Side of the Fence: What Drives Landscape Architecture Now?" *Architectural Record* 188, no. 1 (January 2000): 58–62.

Cerver, Francisco Asensio, and Michael Webb. *Redesigning City Squares and Plazas.* New York: William Morrow & Co., 1997.

Gillette, Jane Brown. "Pure Design, Pure Image." *Landscape Architecture* 88, no. 10 (October 1998): 92–99, 118–20.

Hanson, Steve, ed. "Hargreaves: Landscape Works." *Process: Architecture,* no. 128 (January 1996), entire issue.

Hargreaves, George, and Kendra Taylor. "Prospect Green." *Garten + Landschaft* 106, no. 10 (October 1996): 9–11.

Leviseur, Elsa. "Hargreaves Weaves. George Hargreaves: Projects in California and Other Locations." *The Architectural Review* 193 (December 1993): 80–85.

McGowan, Tempe. "Public Art and the Sydney Olympics: Seeing the City in Its Most Enlivened State." *Sculpture* 19, no. 6 (July/August 2000): 44–49.

Potteiger, Matthew, and Jamie Purinton. *Landscape Narratives: Design Practices for Telling Stories.* New York: John Wiley & Sons, 1998.

Stephens, Suzanne. "The American Campus." *Architectural Record* 189, no. 2 (February 2000): 77–79.

Thompson, J. William. "Metamorphosis." *Landscape Architecture* 89, no. 9 (September 1999): 94–101, 116–18.

HOOD DESIGN

Bennett, Paul. "Hybridizing: Walter Hood Makes His Mark at the Yerba Buena Gardens." *Landscape Architecture* 90, no. 5 (May 2000): 15.

Cutler, Phoebe. "New Angles in Berkeley." *Garden Design* 11, no. 2 (May/June 1992): 42–47.

Hood, Walter. *Walter Hood: Urban Diaries* (*The Land Marks Series, No. 2*), edited by Leah Levy. Washington, D.C.: Spacemaker Press, 1997

———. *Blues & Jazz Landscape Improvisations.* Photographs by Lew Watts. Berkeley, Calif.: Poltroon Press, 1993.

———. "Strengthening a Neighborhood Through Stream Restoration." *Places* 9, no. 3 (Winter 1995): 46.

———. "Documenting Idiosyncrasies: Defining the Multicultural Landscape." In *CITY: Issues of African-American Urban Space.* Baton Rouge, La.: Southern University Graphic Design Publications, 1994.

Hood, Walter et al. *People in a Landscape,* edited by Garrett Eckbo. Upper Saddle River, N.J.: Prentice Hall, 1997.

TOM LEADER STUDIO

Leader, Tom. "City Under Scaffold." *Land Forum,* no. 5 (1999): 90–93.

Project Credits

WIND, SOUND, AND MOVEMENT

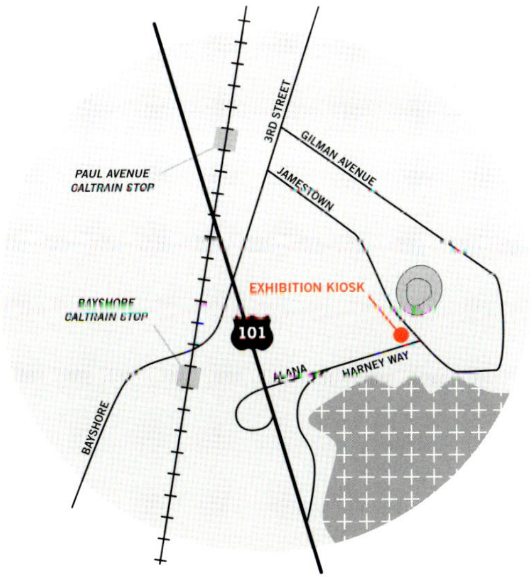

Kathryn Gustafson, **Jaimi Baer** +
Conger Moss Guillard Landscape Architecture
(Kevin Conger, Willett Moss + Chris Guillard)

Location: Harney Way and Jamestown Avenue, Candlestick Point, San Francisco

Major materials: pre-fabricated Mylar spinners, steel rods, corrugated galvanized pipe, plywood, rubber tubing, paint, wind chimes

Acknowledgments: Jack Murphy (International Paragon); John Sanger (Sanger & Olson); Victor McFarlane (Futureplex); Barbra Blake (Barry Friesen Landscape Contractor); White Eagle (Mylar spinner supplier)

MARKINGS

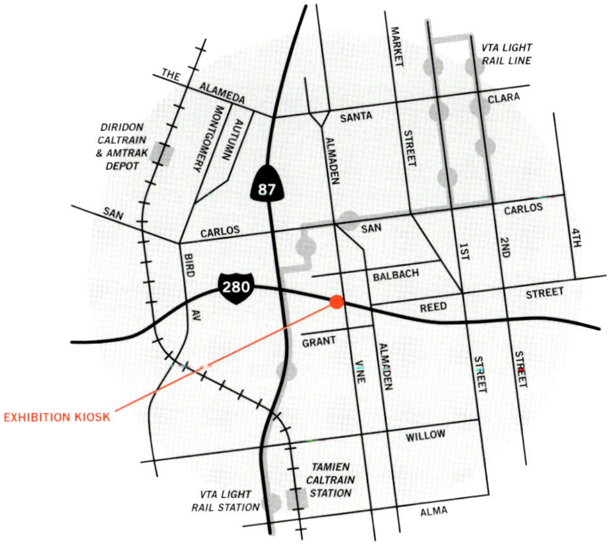

George Hargreaves + **Mary Margaret Jones**
of **Hargreaves Associates**
in collaboration with **Julian Lang**

Location: Intersection of Interstate 280 and Highway 87 (Guadalupe Parkway), San Jose

Major materials: soil, silver paint, black paint

Acknowledgments: P. J. Cosgrove, Eric Foster, and Dave Grubb (Swinerton Builders); Joe Lieber and Herman Ramirez (Caltrans Transportation Art Program); Susan F. Shick, Richard Rios, and Bob Vasquez (San Jose Redevelopment Agency, City of San Jose); Ken Talbot (Architectural Engineering Division of Public Works, City of San Jose); Dr. Gary Lynch (Environmental Services Department, City of San Jose); Susan Landauer (San Jose Museum of Art); Al Longoria (The San Jose Flying Doctors); Bob Reynolds and crew (Reynolds Painting); Phil Marshall (Albanese Construction); Marcel Wilson and Kate Orff (Hargreaves Associates)

LANDSCAPE IN BLUE: ENTROPY IN THE LANDSCAPE

Walter Hood of **Hood Design**
in collaboration with
Olly Wilson + **Douglas Hollis**

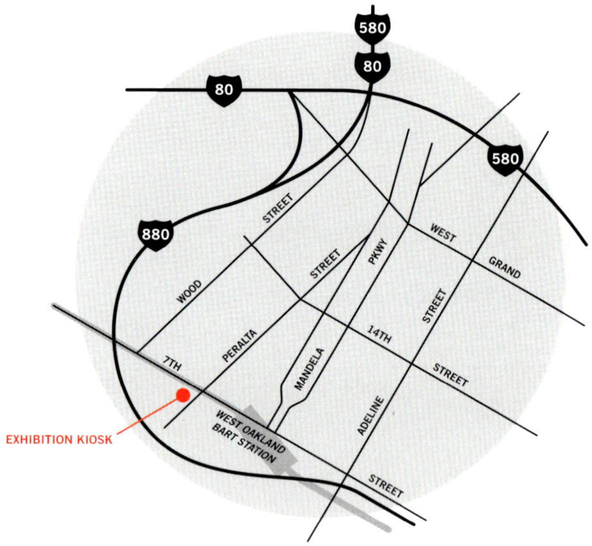

Location: Seventh and Peralta Streets, Oakland

Major materials: benches: wood, integral color concrete, steel, aluminum, Plexiglas, blue shoes, epoxy; reflective panels: Alclad-Aircraft Aluminum, galvanized fabricated steel supports, steel wire and turnbuckles; blue walls: one-by-four-inch pine planks; Douglas fir supports, blue paint

Acknowledgments: Annie Tennant and Philip Vitale (Hood Design); Laura Timothy, Gary Anderson, and Les Freligh (Bay Area Rapid Transit); Kay Barrett (U.S. Post Office); Ben Trautman, Craig Newman, Jane Rongerude, Melissa Erikson, Sophie Robitaille, Alma Luisa De Solier, and Nick (construction team); Ren Bates, Scott Cataffa, Chao-Ti Chen, James Dinh, Anne-Therese Ducrot, Trent Greenan, Haven Kiers, Jennifer Knott, Sandra Koster, Andy Liu, Jeffrey Longhenry, Nathan Lozier, Gabriel Meil, Elisabeth Orr, Edda Ostertag, Zuzana Ponca, Emily Rylander, Derek Schubert, Kirsten Andrea Walker, and Sofia Zander (Master of Landscape Architecture Studio 202, University of California at Berkeley); Anna Murch; Matt Gil Studios

COASTLINES

Tom Leader of **Tom Leader Studio**
in collaboration with
Anuradha Mathur + **Dilip da Cunha**

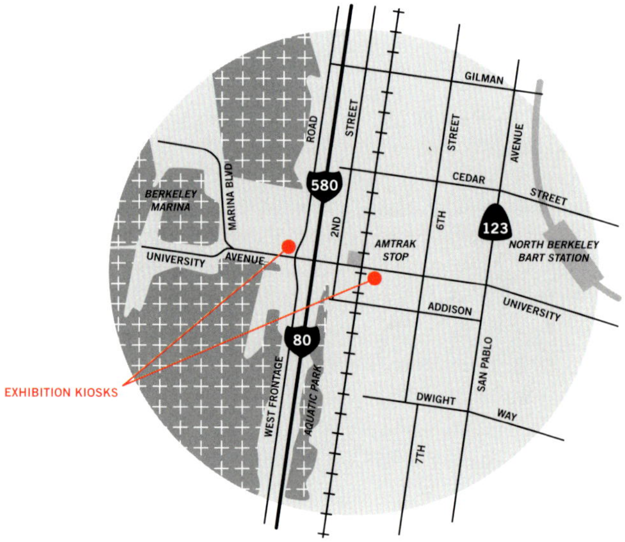

Location: Intersection of Interstate 80 and University Avenue, Berkeley

Major materials: structure: steel rebar, vinyl netting, plastic cable ties; infill: hay, sawdust, oyster shells, ground wood, shoreline detritus, newspaper bundles, shredded paper, shredded cedar, concrete and asphalt chunks, plastic placards, eco-compost, yard waste mulch, plastic bottles, shredded tires, seeds.

Acknowledgments: Angeles Munoz; Guillermo Barbero; Maura Connolly; Philippe Coignet; Mark Liolios (Friends of Aquatic Park); Dana Ellsworth (CLI Commercial Lessors); Steven Block (Steven Block Co.); Alan Yu (Xanadu Restaurant); from the City of Berkeley: Lisa Caronna (Director of Parks and Waterfront); Stuart Sidell (Civic Arts Committee liaison); Maryanne Merker (Civic Arts coordinator); Arietta Chakos (Deputy City Manager); Brad Ricards (Parks Department); Lee Mennell (Public Works Department); Paul Kamen (Waterfront Committee Chair).